THE
DUCHESS OF MALFI

THE
DUCHESS OF MALFI

BY

JOHN WEBSTER

With Introductory essays by GEORGE RYLANDS
and CHARLES WILLIAMS

Illustrated by MICHAEL AYRTON

SYLVAN PRESS

LONDON 1945

PUBLISHERS' NOTE

The text of *The Duchess of Malfi* printed in these pages is that established by Mr F. L. Lucas in his *Complete Works of John Webster* (4 vols.) published by Chatto & Windus, and is here used by kind permission of Editor and Publisher, to both of whom grateful acknowledgement is made. It is a text which records the errors as well as the subtleties of the old printing offices, and is followed exactly in this reprint, save for two or three occasional minute points which a page-design different from that of Mr Lucas's edition has needed to modify: none of noticeable importance. The Editor, in his original preface, writes "the text itself is left as near as possible to the original form in each case; all verbal alterations or additions being enclosed in square brackets". "It is becoming more and more customary", he continues, "in reprinting the older English authors, to keep the old spelling, and though some readers still hate it, I cannot but feel the gain is a real one.... The spelling may often be, as there is reason to think, more the compositor's than the author's: but it is in keeping, and it has an unruly vitality which our stereotyped correctitude has lost." In full memory of Mark Twain's saying that "Chaucer was the worst speller", the Publishers have adopted Mr Lucas's view.

The general arrangement of this reprint has been made by Mr Hubert Foss. It contains two independent essays, one on the production, the other on the poetry, of *The Duchess of Malfi*, contributed respectively by Mr George Rylands and Mr Charles Williams. They present a varied and comprehensive survey of Webster and his work. Where they differ in view the reader will no doubt find argument of greater interest and value than the unmixed praise of appreciation. The type is Monotype Bell, and was chosen not for its "period" but for its suitability to the book's decorations. The pictures that appear in the text are pen-and-ink line drawings.

The limited edition also contains autolithographs by Mr Michael Ayrton which were drawn by the artist direct on to the stones.

MADE IN GREAT BRITAIN

PRINTED BY WALTER LEWIS, M.A., AT THE UNIVERSITY PRESS, CAMBRIDGE

ON THE PRODUCTION OF

The Duchess of Malfi

By George Rylands

Oblivion has blindly scattered her poppy upon all save a mere handful of plays written between the closing of the theatres in 1642 and the impact of Ibsen upon the English drama. Moreover, since the Age of Shakespeare, no English dramatist has succeeded in writing an entirely successful play in verse. From *The Two Tragicall Discourses of Tamburlaine the Great* to the Masque of *Comus*, few dramatists ever thought of employing any other form. Surely this is a very surprising fact. For fifty years dramatist and audience appear to have delighted in this curious baffling hybrid form, poetic drama; and then it expired.

Poets are rare and playwrights rarer; rarest of all is he who identifies both. Where Shakespeare, Sophocles, and Racine triumphed, many a Nicholas Rowe, Matthew Arnold, and Stephen Phillips have failed. But since this is the form in which Shakespeare won immortality and in which Webster chose to compose *The Duchess of Malfi*, the form itself demands a closer investigation. We speak glibly of poetic drama and of dramatic poetry, but we should distinguish more precisely. Without being pedantic or over-subtle, one may say that a poetic drama and a dramatic poem are not quite the same thing. *Romeo and Juliet* is a dramatic poem, *Henry V* a poetic drama. Of course, in the greatest works of art, form and content are "a thing inseparate" like the body and the soul, and in Shakespeare's highest tragedy, *King Lear*, *Othello*, *Macbeth*, and *Antony and Cleopatra*, drama and poem are fused into a single entity. Division

> Admits no orifice for a point as subtle
> As Ariachne's broken woof to enter.

In the succeeding period, Dryden's *All for Love* (1678) is a poetic drama and Milton's *Samson Agonistes* (1671) is a dramatic poem. Later still, Shelley the poet finds expression in *Prometheus Unbound*, Shelley the dramatist in *The Cenci*. *Murder in the Cathedral* is a poetic drama, not a dramatic poem, and it holds the stage.

The distinction which we are pursuing is between the inward essence and the external form. Very few dramatists in verse except Shakespeare, who reached it after trial and error, have achieved this identification in which, in the language of the mediaeval schoolmen, the form *is* the soul. From time to time, in the Elizabethan and Jacobean drama, now for a whole scene, now in an isolated speech, now in a single line, the two arts join hands only to part; and when we close the book or when the curtain falls, we acknowledge a divided response, even a sense of frustration. The fact that some critics have been so misguided as to assert that *King Lear* cannot be acted is in itself evidence enough. Webster comes nearer to fusion than most of his contemporaries but the fusion is fitful. Sometimes the poet speaks, sometimes the dramatist contrives. At his highest moments poetry and drama unite and inter-inanimate each other, like the souls of Donne and his mistress, whence "an abler soul doth flow", or like the marriage of the Phoenix and the Turtle:

> So they lov'd, as love in twain
> Had the essence but in one;
> Two distincts, division none:
> Number there in love was slain.

Poets are seldom plotters, and plot, according to Aristotle, is the soul of tragedy. Webster could handle a scene but he could not compass a plot. Second to plot, and subservient to it, is character. Character in drama—*a fortiori* in poetic drama—is so restricted in function that it stands to the psychological creations of the novelist as a charcoal sketch to a portrait in oils. "Outside Shakespeare and perhaps Ben Jonson", writes Virginia Woolf, "there are no characters in Elizabethan drama, only violences whom we know so little that we can scarcely care what becomes of them." She goes on to compare the Annabella of John Ford with Anna Karenina:

The Russian woman is flesh and blood, nerves and temperament, has heart, brain, body and mind where the English girl is flat and crude as a face painted on a playing card; she is without depth, without range, without intricacy. But as we say this we know that we have missed something. We have let the meaning of the play slip through our hands. We have ignored the emotion which has been accumulating because it has accumulated in places where we have not expected to find it. We have been comparing the play with prose and after all the play is poetry....

The extremes of passion are not for the novelist; the perfect marriages of sense and sound are not for him; he must tame his swiftness to sluggardry; keep his eyes on the ground, not on the sky: suggest by description not reveal by illumination....Granted all the little dexterities by which the novelist makes us know the individual and recognize the real, the dramatist goes beyond the single and the separate, shows us not Annabella in love, but love itself; not Anna Karenina throwing herself under the train, but ruin and death and the

> ...soul, like to a ship in a black storm
> ...driven, I know not whither.

All that Mrs Woolf has to say in her admirable Notes on *'Tis Pity She's a Whore* applies to *The Duchess of Malfi*. Webster's characters, where they exist within their own convention, are at least one remove from those of Shakespeare, as those of Shakespeare are at least one remove from the characters of Tolstoi and of Henry James. But again and again they seem of a sudden to possess hypnotic gifts and to be inspired with the Ancient Mariner's strange power of speech:

> Forthwith this frame of mine was wrench'd
> With a woful agony,
> Which forced me to begin my tale;
> And then it left me free.
>
> Since then, at an uncertain hour,
> That agony returns:
> And till my ghastly tale is told,
> This heart within me burns.

Such are the suddenness, the uncertainty, and the burning agony of Webster's creatures and when the moment comes he holds us with his glittering eye. The Mariner hath his will.

In 1510, Giovanna, aged twenty-two, grand-daughter of Ferdinand I of Naples, of the house of Aragon, and widow of Alfonso Piccolomini, first Duke of Amalfi, fled with the major-domo of her household, Antonio Bologna, to Ancona. Her brothers, Lodovico Cardinal of Aragon and the Duke Carlo, avenged the stain upon their honour. The Duchess separated herself from Antonio for his greater safety, was taken prisoner and immured in a castle of her Duchy, and was never heard of again. More than a year later, Antonio, ignorant of her fate, was stabbed on his way to Mass by Daniel da Bozolo, a Lombard Captain. The story is told by Bandello, who passed Antonio in the street a few moments before he was assassinated. He had heard it from a Neapolitan *condottiere*, a man hired to commit the murder, who had instead warned Antonio of his danger. Belleforest translated the tale in his *Histoires Tragiques* (1566) and a year later it was translated from the French by William Painter in his *Palace of Pleasure*. "And so", says Mr F. L. Lucas, "through the hands of a gentleman, a fool, and a knave the tale reached Webster."

The play, if we ignore the Act and Scene divisions as in the Elizabethan Drama we nearly always should, falls, as they nearly always do, into three movements. The first movement ends after Act II with the resolve of Ferdinand, the Great Duke of Calabria:

> Till I know who leapes my sister, i'll not stirre;
> That knowne, i'll finde Scorpions to string my whips,
> And fix her in a generall ecclipse.

The movement falls into two halves. In the first, the personalities of the Duchess and of her two brothers, of Bosola and Antonio, are strongly rather than subtly stated. The Duke and the Cardinal forbid her to marry again, and, within a few moments, she has summoned Antonio, the Master of her Household, and offered him her heart and hand. This proposal scene is handled with great delicacy and is very lovely. It is one of those rare gleams of pale sunshine which break through the thunder clouds of Webster's tragic sky. The chorus-ending spoken by Cariola, her maid, foretells the storm, sums up the character of the heroine, and signifies the nature of our response to the drama:

> Whether the spirit of greatnes, or of woman
> Raigne most in her, I know not, but it shewes
> A fearfull madnes. I owe her much of pitty.

Characterization, of course, in any modern sense, we must not seek for too diligently. Poetic drama dispenses with it. From the materials of *Hamlet* and *Macbeth* we may fashion delusively life-like figures, but the poet's imagination aspires to create "forms more real than living man, nurslings of immortality". Cariola tells us all we need to know of the Duchess. Antonio has already celebrated her with the hyperbole and exaltation of the Elizabethan sonneteers:

> Let all sweet Ladies breake their flattring Glasses,
> And dresse themselves in her.

His panegyric is uttered while the Duchess and her court are on the stage; and the characters of her brothers, who are also present, are no less obligingly communicated by Antonio. It is a crude and amateurish device which puts the producer in a fix; but Antonio is a shrewd commentator and hits off Ferdinand succinctly:

> a most perverse, and turbulent Nature—
> What appeares in him mirth, is meerely outside;
> If he laugh hartely, it is to laugh
> All honesty out of fashion.

Bosola is also introduced by a "programme note" from Antonio on his first entry, but in the brief dialogue which immediately follows and his short vigorous interchange with Ferdinand, leading up to "I am your creature", Bosola rapidly acquaints us with his individual idiom. If we do not *know* him, we *feel* him, which for the dramatist is all that matters. Indeed, by the end of the first act, we *feel* all the chief personalities individually, despite that curiosity of expression which they all have in common.

In the second half of the first movement the plot accelerates. Bosola guesses that the Duchess is with child:

> I have a tricke, may chance discover it
> (A pretty one)—I have bought some Apricocks,
> The first our Spring yeelds.

She is secretly delivered of a boy and Bosola picks up a paper dropped by Antonio, in which the child's nativity is calculated, but which does not name the father. He despatches the news to the Cardinal in Rome, and after a brief scene which introduces Julia, the Cardinal's mistress, who has an important part to play in the fourth act, we reach the climax of the first movement, Ferdinand's revelation to the Cardinal of their sister's shame and disobedience. This is as powerful a scene as Webster ever wrote, and highly characteristic of his extraordinary style. The two voices contrast and blend and draw apart as the high vibrant notes of a fiddle strain and soar above the still, chill chords of a pianoforte accompaniment.

The martyrdom of the Duchess fills the second movement. There is a last momentary gleam of sunshine when wife and husband and maid tease one another in the Duchess's bedchamber. While she is doing her hair, they steal away and leave her talking to herself. Ferdinand comes from behind the arras and, as she laughingly says the words,

> You shall get no more children till my brothers
> Consent to be your Ghossips,

she beholds her brother in the mirror and turns to face the dagger which he holds towards her. It is a tense dramatic moment. Webster rises to it with mastery and ease in some sixty-five lines in which passionate emotion and imaginative utterance are lightened with touches of strange fantasy and resolved in the pure poetry of the fable of Reputation, Love, and Death. His insertion of the fable of the Salmon and the Dog-fish soon after, to close the third act when the Duchess is taken prisoner, is harder to justify in the theatre, but it creates and communicates the Duchess's mood of resignation and endurance.

The horrors of the fourth act have been dismissed as *Grand Guignol*. The *virtu* of the Duchess—in the old sense of the word— the innate yet more than human quality—is subjected to the ingenious Renaissance cruelties of her brother, the grotesque clowning of the concourse of madmen and the process of gradual mortification conducted by Bosola in the disguise of an ancient maker of tombs. In such a setting it shines out "like a star i'th' darkest night", the precious jewel in the head of an ugly and venomous toad. The scene is mediaeval as a Dance of Death. Webster prepares and places his climaxes with instinctive skill: "Who am I?... Am not I thy duchess?... I am Duchess of Malfi still": the Dirge: the execution of the Duchess without a cry—"strangling is a very quiet death"; the shrill scream of Cariola, "I am quick with child", and Bosola's sardonic retort, "Why, then, your credit's saved": Ferdinand's entrance and the everlasting epitaph which he speaks: "Cover her face; mine eyes dazzle; she died young": the sudden quickening of the tempo, when the murderer wrangles with his hired tool; the revulsion of feeling on the part of both; the incipient madness of the Duke following so hard upon his crime, as with the *Orestes* of Aeschylus; the momentary recovery of the Duchess; Bosola's honourable lie and his vow of repentance: this whole extraordinary sequence not only expresses (in Hazlitt's words) "the writhing and conflict and sublime colloquy of man's nature with itself", but also shows that when the demand was greatest, Webster's genius could achieve the complete identification of poetry and drama.

After such an achievement it is inevitable that the last movement which fills the fifth act may prove an anticlimax, and it sets a problem for the producer. The same problem is posed by the last two acts of *Julius Cæsar* and of *King Lear*; more fatally still in *Macbeth*. The madness of Ferdinand, the Julia episode, the eighteenth-century "Gothick" interlude of the Echo scene, the inspired and startling images which always rise to the lips of Webster's characters in their death agony—all these things, effective though they are, fail to set the last movement of *The Duchess of Malfi* on a level with the grand dénouement and finale of Webster's twin masterpiece, *The White Divel*. The difference between them is the difference between the Duchess herself and her twin, the Great Duke. *The Duchess of Malfi* is in a minor, *The White Divel* in a major key. "We think cag'd birds sing when indeed they cry", Flamineo says in the latter play, but the cry of the imprisoned Duchess is lyrical. Vittoria compels our admiration, as she does that of her brother, but our response to her tragic story is best expressed in Albany's comment on Goneril's murder of her sister and of herself;

> This judgement of the heavens, that makes us tremble,
> Touches us not with pity.

In *The Duchess of Malfi* our compassion is aroused not only by Antonio (who at moments, it must be confessed, cannot be acquitted of feebleness) and by his Duchess, but also by Bosola, divided against himself, an adventurer with a little of Brutus in him; yes, even by Ferdinand, driven by some relentless force in himself, some fever of the blood, which he cannot comprehend—"a hollow bullet filled with unquenchable wild-fire". As has been said, the creatures of poetic drama are not "characters" in any strict sense of the word; Webster's less so than many. They are elemental. Beside them Hamlet and Cleopatra are as realistic as Falstaff and Mistress Quickly. But even Cleopatra when she dies, says

> I am fire and air; my baser elements
> I give to baser life,....

and we recall Marlowe's

> Nature that framed us of four elements
> Warring within our breast for regiment....

Elizabethan "characterization" was founded upon the schematized physiology *cum* psychology of mediaeval thought. Ferdinand and his twin sister are respectively "fire" and "air". The Cardinal and Bosola are the baser elements. The Cardinal is all ice; Bosola is of the earth, earthy. "Of the earth, earthy" is Charles Lamb's comment on the dirge in *The White Divel*, and he pairs it with the ditty, "of the water, watery", which in *The Tempest* reminds Ferdinand of his drowned father. "Both have that intenseness of feeling", Lamb concludes, "which seems to resolve itself into the element which it contemplates". Such is the intensity of Webster's imagination and of his creatures.

A modern actor, however, cast for the part of Ferdinand, will not be much helped or encouraged if he is told that he must impersonate an element. Characterization in the theatre to-day has separated and stabilized itself into various easily recognizable types, which trace their pedigree to the days of Pinero, and which have acquired a certain amount of education from the novel, the short story, the comic papers, and so forth. Apart from our talented "character actors", the heroes and heroines execute as often as not variations on a too familiar theme. And then of course there is Shakespeare. His dramatic roles inspire naïve enthusiasm and innocent awe; and in the hearts of producer and actor, inarticulate and incurious, there abides the oracular axiom: "After all, Shakespeare is Shakespeare and blank verse is blank verse." Whether the play be *Richard III* or *The Winter's Tale* is all one, and as for blank verse, it can be taken very fast or it can be taken very slow; it can be spouted or distilled; disguised as prose so that the audience cry "How modern!", or recited as an incantation so that they feel themselves to be participating in a religious rite. Although this is what usually happens in actual performance, it is only fair to say that the Shakespearean actor desires to "realize" the character which he has to play, and fabricates for his own purposes, as conscientiously as A. C. Bradley, an interpretation which is psychologically consistent and recognizably life-like. In the case of Shakespeare, for good or ill, this can undoubtedly be done. In Webster and his contemporaries, it as certainly can not.

Nor on the other hand do the language and versification of Webster lend themselves either to the traditional or to the fashionable method of the Shakespearean stage. They can neither be intoned nor "thrown away". What then shall the actor do to be saved? The answer is simple. He must learn a new language. He must master the Elizabethan and Jacobean idiom. He will not learn it from Shakespeare, although once he has learnt it he will begin to do justice to Shakespeare's style. But he will learn it everywhere else; in the prose no less than the poetry; in song and sonnet as well as in the drama; in the sermons and translations and essays and novels and pamphlets and pastoral romances; in Donne and Spenser and Lyly and Bacon and Marston and North and Campion and Earle and the Authorized Version. The language of Webster is "everything by starts and nothing long".

His range is extensive. The pervading tone is macabre, shadowed with the melancholy of the disillusioned Jaques:

It is a melancholy of mine own, compounded of many simples, extracted from many objects, and indeed the sundry contemplation of my travels, which, by often rumination, wraps me in a most humourous sadness.

But he is more of a scholar than Jaques, the sometime libertine, and his travels have been in the realms of gold, the world of books. Webster continually surprises us by eccentricity or excess, for example in

> We had need goe borrow that fantastique glasse
> Invented by *Galileo* the Florentine,
> To view another spacious world i' th' Moone,
> And looke to find a constant woman there.

or

> Me thinkes I see her laughing,
> Excellent Hyenna!

or

Thou art a box of worm-seede, at best but a salvatory of greene mummey: what's this flesh? a little cruded milke, phantasticall puffe-paste.

or   What would it pleasure me, to have my throate cut
              With diamonds? or to be smothered
              With Cassia? or to be shot to death, with pearles?
              I know death hath ten thousand severall doores
              For men, to take their *Exits*; and 'tis found
              They go on such strange geometricall hinges,
              You may open them both wayes.

or   Give me some wet hay, I am broken-winded—
              I do account this world but a dog-kennell:
              I will vault credit, and affect high pleasures,
              Beyond death.

But there is much else besides the fits and starts of passion, the wayward flights of fancy. There are simplicity and the speaking voice:

              What is't distracts you? This is flesh and blood, (Sir)
              'Tis not the figure cut in Allablaster
              Kneeles at my husbands tombe. Awake, awake (man)
              I do here put off all vaine ceremony,
              And onely doe appeare to you a yong widow
              That claimes you for her husband, and like a widow,
              I use but halfe a blush in't.

In the Proposal scene and in the Echo scene there are sustained writing and verbal melody. And then again, from time to time a cry breaks from the heart:

              O that it were possible we might
              But hold some two dayes conference with the dead.

and   that we cannot be suffer'd
              To doe good when we have a mind to it!

and   'Tis weakenesse,
              Too much to think what should have bin done—I go,
              I know not whither.

If Webster's style is a stumbling-block, his versification cannot be said to assist the actor to circumvent it. The verse is extremely resolved and irregular, so that the beat is easily lost; there are many half-lines; and the end of the decasyllable is seldom marked by a pause in the sense, except where the expression is sententious and the versification shifts to the other extreme of formalization, including the use of the couplet. The arbitrary intervention of prose adds to the confusion. In consequence, the general impression resembles the broken rhythms of rhetorical prose or of free verse. The peculiar effect may not be deliberate but it has its value. The sudden striking phrases flash out with greater brilliance from a background of moving cloud. In this half-world between poetry and prose, the tragedy has a dream-like quality. As in a nightmare we are conscious, now of a fearful urgency, and now of timelessness. Words and images become more memorable than the situations which excite them or the passions which they express. They acquire an imaginative significance which

> apprehends
> More than cool reason ever comprehends.

Our response to *The Duchess of Malfi* is more emotional than to *The White Divel*. The latter play is more gnomic and thus sets the audience at a distance. We are fascinated but detached. The suffering of the Duchess and the conflict in the breast of Bosola and of Ferdinand wring the heart. Terror and pity, the two emotions which Aristotle affirms are proper to tragedy, are commingled, and heighten one another. The play is at once a dramatic poem and a poetic drama, and the fusion has been achieved by the uniqueness of Webster's utterance, by his startling metaphor and simile, by his strange juxtapositions, by his incorporation of phrases and fancies borrowed from other writers, and by his ear. He is at the same time essentially Jacobean, with that profound mediaeval strain which we find in John Donne, and exceptionally individual. *The Duchess of Malfi* is as great a tragedy as any outside Shakespeare. By savouring it in the study or experiencing it upon the stage, we can gauge the unlikeness of Shakespeare to his contemporaries, modern where they are mediaeval, homely where they are eccentric, self-taught where they are scholarly, wise with the wisdom of the ale-house and the market-place rather than learned in the ways of the Court and Council, in the ante-chambers of the great and the solitude of books.

ON THE POETRY OF
The Duchess of Malfi

By CHARLES WILLIAMS

The Dutchesse of Malfy is thought to have been written about 1613–14. Webster was then a man of thirty-four or so; he had collaborated with other dramatists in various comedies and had finished Marston's *Malcontent* for the stage in 1604. *The White Divel* had been produced in 1608. By 1613–14 the Queen had been dead ten years. It was twenty since Marlowe had been stabbed at Deptford. Shakespeare was living in retirement at Stratford, having finished *The Tempest* about a year earlier, and being now (or a little before or after) engaged on his part of *Henry VIII*. Jonson was still in his full powers; *The Alchemist* had appeared some four years earlier, and *Bartholomew Fair* was almost contemporary with the *Dutchesse*. Chapman had finished most of his work. Tourneur's *Revenger's Tragedy* had been published in 1607. Fletcher, Massinger, and Ford were still to do much work; Ford indeed practically all his. *The Changeling* was to come in 1623. But the hour of that grand style had almost passed.

The *Dutchesse* is not on the level of *The White Divel*. It is almost permissible to see it as the very point of lessening of that tragic imagination which we call, roughly, Elizabethan. A phrase from the late and lonely terror of *The Changeling* may serve to mark the difference between the two periods, and perhaps even between *The White Divel* and the *Dutchesse*. In Middleton's play (III, iii) the murderer De Flores says to Beatrice who has employed him:

> Push! Flye not to your birth, but settle you
> In what the act has made you; y'are no more now.
> You must forget your parentage to me,
> Y'are the deeds creature, by that name
> You lost your first condition, and I challenge you,
> As peace and innocency has turn'd you out,
> And made you one with me.

The phrase "You are the deed's creature" creates distinction between Elizabethan tragedies. It can be used as a measure; we can see by it what certain plays do and others do not do. *Hamlet* is hardly covered by it; the Prince, for good or evil, has no deed of which he can properly be called a creature; and Claudius is certainly

not treated seriously as a creature of his. But *Macbeth* is precisely
a play of this kind; it is in the fore-dooming, "We still have judge-
ments here". *The Revenger's Tragedy* is too wildly hideous a discord
to bear any so composed an inevitability; it is its very character that
anything may happen, and its effects are by no means so certainly
within their causes. There is more of that inevitable doom, that
natural judgement, in *The White Divel*, though it is postponed till
the last scene. Vittoria, till then, remains magnificent; in the great
act of the trial she dominates her deeds as she does her accusers.
Her vitality thrives in her deeds, as Iago's does in his. Yet her
dying phrase has something of that other sense:

> My soule, like to a ship in a black storme
> Is driven I know not whither.

Her creatureliness begins to be known to her. Flamineo, her
brother, is spared even that, but then he is hardly of importance till
his end. Webster found the greatest phrases for his people precisely
as they approach their end. In Mr Eliot's lines

> He knew that thought clings round dead limbs
> Tightening its lusts and luxuries.

Only something of this is true of the *Dutchesse*. It is necessary to
decide in which of two ways to regard it. The first is to see it as
mainly about the Duchess herself, with the last act forming a kind
of—perhaps superfluous—epilogue. The second is to see the last act
as a necessary part of the play; by which reading the Duchess becomes a less important figure and the title an accident. There is,
I think, no real doubt which is preferable, if possible. One should
always begin by assuming that any play—indeed, any book—was
meant to have the shape it has. It may prove impossible to main-
tain this, or one may be driven to judge the shape a bad shape.
Julius Cæsar has been an example of the difficulty; many readers
have in fact come to believe that it has no outline or at best "a
demn'd outline". I think it has a shape, but this is no place to
defend it. The *Dutchesse* certainly has a firmer exterior shape, if not
so intense an imaginative unity. It has a shape, but it is hardly an
organism except in its spasmodic and convulsive movements of
great poetry.

In this it differs from its greater predecessor, *The White Divel*.
There the Elizabethan convention of the daring, lecherous, and
destructive spirit was given full play. The victims were inserted,
and scarcely even that. But here much is made of the victims, and
the destroyers scarcely begin to be important until their murder is

achieved. Ferdinand has indeed something of life in the scene when
he leaves the knife with his sister, but the Cardinal incarnates only
by his fishpools; he is that at which the thing armed with a rake
strikes upward, and he is a man only so. But sufficiently. There is
hardly a better example of the way in which poetry creates characters, rather than (as we so habitually tend to think) that the
characters independently exist and talk poetry. The imagined
murderers of this play are, in a less moral and more purely
dramatic sense than Middleton meant, "the deed's creatures". It
lies somewhere between *The Changeling* and *The Revenger's Tragedy*
in weight of significance; as it does between *The White Divel* and
The Devil's Law Case in chronological lessening of force. Webster's
own genius was dissolving; I do not say it was less, but it was less
determined. This is a play of mirrors, and the mirrors are curved,
so that the figures are out of proportion. It does not perhaps matter
much that the two brothers should seem to have no adequate
motive for their murdered sister; we are used to that among the
Elizabethans. Passion is continually seeking for a cause, as Iago's
is. But it seems strange that Webster should have done no more
for Antonio. The figure of the lover in him is thin and wavering;
was it for this that the Duchess outraged her house by misalliance?
He is a wraith by her, and wanders helplessly among things too
high for him.

Bosola himself is something of a wraith. He says to Ferdinand:
"I am your creature", but this creatureliness is not active either in
deeds or in apprehension. The present writer remembers, at an
early age, reading this play among others in a great green volume
called *British Dramatists*, which ranged from Lyly to Shirley, and
then seeing Bosola as an old crooked man, full of wicked malice,
introducing madmen and murderers into the Duchess's chamber.
It was the inaccurate reading of a boy, but it was a tribute to the
general effect of the play that it should so transform the figure, and
now I a little regret my earlier Bosola. This Melancholy, till the
last act, does so little. He drifts in and out, helpless and "intelligencing"—that is, spying. It is all he is given to do. But it is
astonishing that, in his first great scene with the Duchess, he should
be given no more to say.

> DUTCH. What are you? (*she turns suddenly to a Servant*)
> SER. One that wishes you long life.
> DUTCH. I would thou wert hang'd for the horrible curse
> Thou hast given me: I shall shortly grow one
> Of the miracles of pitty: I'll goe pray: No,
> I'll goe curse:

BOS. Oh fye!

DUTCH. I could curse the Starres.

BOS. Oh fearefull!

DUTCH. And those three smyling seasons of the yeere
Into a Russian winter: nay the world
To its first Chaos.

BOS. Looke you, the Starres shine still:

DUTCH. Oh, but you must remember, my curse hath a great way to goe:
Plagues, (that make lanes through largest families)
Consume them!

BOS. Fye lady!

DUTCH. Let them like tyrants
Never be remembred, but for the ill they have done:
Let all the zealous prayers of mortefied
Church-men forget them—

BOS. O uncharitable!

DUTCH. Let heaven, a little while, cease crowning Martirs
To punish them:
Goe, howle them this: and say I long to bleed—
"It is some mercy, when men kill with speed."

We must suppose the interjections meant so, but it seems an ill-judgement, for even the Duchess's agony loses something of itself in such a void.

As if Webster had been conscious of some weakness in Bosola here, he concentrated more power on him in the next scene, both in prose and verse; it is this which goes to make the death of the Duchess terrible, for the madmen are only just gone and the murderers are to come, and the Duchess is not allowed to have her own moments uncommented. The scene must be read in its place; but one phrase is worth remembering here. When the Duchess exclaims, in six often-quoted words: "I am Duchesse of *Malfy* still", Bosola counters, with awful lucidity, in another six not so often quoted: "That makes thy sleepes so broken." It is in this fourth act that the play, as we say, "comes to life"; that is, it becomes, after its own kind, credible; which again means that we are satisfied with the words, "felt in the blood and felt along the heart". These revelations of the soul are at once thrilling and composing.

It is however Bosola who twice uses a word, which is once repeated by the Duchess, and (so repeated) seems to define the earlier part of the play; it is the word *dung*. The full sentence of which part was quoted above in the allusion to Bosola's creatureliness (I, i) is:

What's my place?
The Provisor-ship o' the horse? say then my corruption
Grew out of horse-doong: I am your creature.

There is, so early, already a kind of corpse-light over this germi-
nating dung. In the second act (ii, i), when he brings the Duchess
apricots in order to find out her condition, and she eats them, he says:

> DUCH. Indeed I thank you: they are wondrous faire ones:
> What an unskilfull fellow is our Gardiner!
> We shall have none this moneth.
> BOS. Will not your Grace pare them?
> DUCH. No, they tast of muske (me thinkes) indeed they doe:
> BOS. I know not: yet I wish your Grace had parde 'em:
> DUCH. Why?
> BOS. I forgot to tell you the knave Gardner,
> (Onely to raise his profit by them the sooner)
> Did ripen them in horse-doung.
> DUCH. O you jest.

This recurrence of the word at such a point of his "intelligencing"
increases the sense of a corruption nursing the good; so that the
Duchess's own pregnancy has this spiritual evil about it. Then, in
the fourth act (iv, i), it occurs again, after the Duchess has seen the
wax figures of her husband and children:

> BOS. Looke you: here's the peece, from which 'twas ta'ne:
> He doth present you this sad spectacle,
> That now you know directly they are dead,
> Hereafter you may (wisely) cease to grieve
> For that which cannot be recovered.
> DUCH. There is not betweene heaven, and earth one wish
> I stay for after this: it wastes me more,
> Then were't my picture, fashion'd out of wax,
> Stucke with a magicall needle, and then buried
> In some fowle dung-hill.

But now the dung and the corruption are one. Her phrase does but
describe what is happening; the play is exactly her image buried
in a dung-hill.

It is true that at first it is perhaps too well buried. In the apricot
scene Bosola says of her: "How greedily she eats them!" She is
eating her bane, but that touch of greediness is also her bane, and
has been. There are various opinions of her love-scenes. I have
known women who rejected them from no prudery. She is no
Miranda or Imogen; her love-scenes have no touch of illumination,
and the fact that she is a widow and a mother is mentioned too often
for it to be forgotten. Even if the scene of her wooing be accepted,
her later passages of love with Antonio would be more delightful
without the slight vulgarity. It is no question of mere sex.
Vittoria—and Miranda and Imogen—had that. It is perhaps
(iii, ii) the presence of the waiting-maid Cariola that helps to spoil

it, and Antonio's not very amusing trick on his wife. The scene waits for Ferdinand to change it; but at least it is the Duchess whose words, when she so suddenly sees him, do so.

> Tis welcome:
> For know whether I am doomb'd to live or die,
> I can do both like a Prince.

It is he who, speaking of her and to her, uses words which re-define the corruption. He says (III, ii)

> Pursue thy wishes:
> And glory in them: there's in shame no comfort,
> But to be past all bounds, and sense of shame.

But, in a sense beyond Ferdinand's, this is what he and the Cardinal, so far as they have been anything, have already always been. From now on, that lack of shame is open and exposed everywhere. The Duchess herself is not left quite free from it. When she is planning an escape (III, ii), Bosola suggests that she shall pretend piety:

> BOS. Let me thinke:
> I would wish your Grace, to faigne a Pilgrimage
> To our Lady of *Loretto* (scarce seaven leagues
> From faire *Ancona*)—so may you depart
> Your Country, with more honour, and your flight
> Will seeme a Princely progresse, retaining
> Your usuall traine about you.
> DUCH. Sir, your direction
> Shall lead me, by the hand.
> CAR. In my opinion,
> She were better progresse to the bathes at *Leuca*,
> Or go visit the *Spaw*
> In *Germany*, for (if you will beleeve me)
> I do not like this jesting with religion,
> This faigned Pilgrimage.
> DUCH. Thou art a superstitious foole,
> Prepare us instantly for our departure.

It is true the pretence has been pressed on her, yet her answer does her no good with us. Some momentary hesitation would have saved all. It is however in the next scene that the persons of Ferdinand and the Cardinal begin to stand out, when the Cardinal "lifts up's nose", and "the Lord Ferdinand laughs". The murders are accomplished in the next act, and when the bodies of the children are shown to Ferdinand his own madness first begins to peep out (IV, ii):

> The death
> Of young Wolffes is never to be pittied.

He follows it with a borrowing from *The White Divel*:

> The Wolfe shall finde her Grave, and scrape it up:
> Not to devour the corpses, but to discover
> The horrid murther.

This is an echo of

> But keep the Wolf from hence, that's foe to men,
> Or with his nails he'll dig them up again.

There are two or three such repetitions in this play, but generally of a lowered force. When Cariola (iv, ii) says to the Duchess: "What thinke you of, Madam?" she answers:

> Of nothing.
> When I muse thus, I sleepe.

It is the changed: "Nothing; of nothing; leave thy idle questions" of Flamineo (*White Divel*, v, i). And the unfortunate and unnecessary Julia (v, ii), dying by poison, says:

> I go,
> I know not whither;

which is but an echo of Vittoria's cry.

The word "echo" brings us back to its use in the *Dutchesse*, in the third scene of the fifth act. This is perhaps the most purely moving scene which the Duchess has. Her earthly greatness has ended—royalty and courage alike. She is not even required to make another entry as a ghost. Webster would not so enliven death; it would have too much broken up his bloody and again corrupting earth. She is not even an echo, but "there is an Eccho (from the Dutchesse Grave)". Its first sound is the reverberation of "like death that we have"; its last, "Never see her more"; and it is almost the only beauty in those last acts of madness and death. Against it, the Cardinal's speech stands out (v, v), like hell against death, worse life against loss of life:

> CARD. I am puzzell'd in a question about hell:
> He saies, in hell, there's one materiall fire,
> And yet it shall not burne all men alike.
> Lay him by: How tedious is a guilty conscience!
> When I looke into the Fish-ponds, in my Garden,
> Me thinkes I see a thing, arm'd with a Rake
> That seemes to strike at me:
> (*Enter Bosola and Servant bearing Antonio's body.*)
> Now? art thou come? thou look'st ghastly:
> There sits in thy face, some great determination,
> Mix'd with some feare.

The end is, one might think, deliberately grotesque. Ferdinand's lycanthropy—say, his wolf-nature—has reached its height in the speech in v, ii.

> One met the Duke, 'bout midnight in a lane
> Behind St. *Markes* Church, with the leg of a man
> Upon his shoulder; and he howl'd fearfully:
> Said he was a Woolffe: onely the difference
> Was, a Woolffes skinne was hairy on the out-side,
> His on the In-side: bad them take their swords,
> Rip up his flesh, and trie.

After that the wantonness and assassinations are all but a wearisomeness; the Echo sounds sadly and pitifully among them, and then they begin again. At last, the death-scuffle between the Cardinal, the mad Duke, and Bosola takes place almost under the eyes of a deceived and amused Court. It is proper. They die without many great phrases; the Cardinal indeed without any. Ferdinand has his

> I do account this world but a dog-kennell:
> I will vault credit, and affect high pleasures,
> Beyond death.

But it is Bosola who sums up the play. It is almost like him; it also holds its weary soul in its teeth. All the lords, and all love and greatness, now

> end in a little point, a kind of nothing.

What then?

> Oh this gloomy world,
> In what a shadow, or deepe pit of darknesse,
> Doth (womanish and fearefull) mankind live.

DRAMATIS PERSONAE

BOSOLA

FERDINAND

CARDINALL

ANTONIO

DELIO

FOROBOSCO

MALATESTE

The MARQUESSE *of* PES-
CARA

SILVIO

(CASTRUCHIO)

(RODERIGO)

(GRISOLAN)

The SEVERALL MAD MEN

The DUTCHESSE

The CARDINALS

The DOCTOR

CARIOLA

COURT OFFICERS

(OLD LADY)

THREE YOUNG CHILDREN

TWO PILGRIMS

(LADIES, EXECUTIONERS,
and ATTENDANTS)

Actus Primus.   Scena Prima

[Amalfi. The Palace of the Duchess]

[Enter Antonio and Delio]

DELIO

Y ou are wel-come to your Country (deere *Antonio*)
   You have bin long in *France,* and you returne
   A very formall French-man, in your habit.
How doe you like the French Court?
      ANTONIO. I admire it—
In seeking to reduce both State, and People
To a fix'd Order, the[ir] juditious King
Begins at home; Quits first his Royall Pallace
Of flattring Sicophants, of dissolute,
And infamous persons—which he sweetely termes
His Masters Master-peece (the worke of Heaven)
Considring duely, that a Princes Court
Is like a common Fountaine, whence should flow
Pure silver-droppes in generall: But if 't chance
Some curs'd example poyson't neere the head,
"Death, and diseases through the whole land spread.
And what is't makes this blessed government,
But a most provident Councell, who dare freely
Informe him the corruption of the times?
Though some oth'Court hold it presumption
To instruct Princes what they ought to doe,

It is a noble duety to informe them
What they ought to fore-see: Here comes *Bosola*   [*enter Bosola*
The onely Court-Gall: yet I observe his rayling
Is not for simple love of Piety:
Indeede he rayles at those things which he wants,
Would be as leacherous, covetous, or proud,
Bloody, or envious, as any man,
If he had meanes to be so: Here's the Cardinall   [*enter Cardinal*

BOSOLA. I doe haunt you still.

CARDINALL. So.

BOSOLA. I have done you better service then to be slighted thus:
miserable age, where onely the reward of doing well, is the doing
of it!

CARDINALL. You inforce your merrit to[o] much.

BOSOLA. I fell into the Gallies in your service, where, for two
yeares together, I wore two Towells in stead of a shirt, with a
knot on the shoulder, after the fashion of a Romaine Mantle:
Slighted thus? I will thrive some way: black-birds fatten best in
hard weather: why not I, in these dogge dayes?

CARDINALL. Would you could become honest—

BOSOLA. With all your divinity, do but direct me the way to it
—I have knowne many travell farre for it, and yet returne as arrant
knaves, as they went forth; because they carried themselves alwayes
along with them; [*exit Cardinal*] Are you gon? Some fellowes (they
say) are possessed with the divell, but this great fellow, were able
to possesse the greatest Divell, and make him worse.

ANTONIO. He hath denied thee some suit?

BOSOLA. He, and his brother, are like Plum-trees (that grow
crooked over standing-pooles) they are rich, and ore-laden with
Fruite, but none but Crowes, Pyes, and Catter-pillers feede on
them: Could I be one of their flattring Panders, I would hang on
their eares like a horse-leach, till I were full, an[d] then droppe off:
I pray leave me.
    Who wold relie upon these miserable dependances, in expecta-
tion to be advanc'd to-morrow? what creature ever fed worse,
then hoping *Tantalus*? nor ever di[e]d any man more fearefully,
then he that hop'd for a p[ar]don: There are rewards for hawkes,
and dogges, when they have done us service; but for a Souldier,
that hazards his Limbes in a battaile, nothing but a kind of
Geometry, is his last Supportation.

DELIO. Geometry?

BOSOLA. I, to hang in a faire paire of slings, take his latter-
swinge in the world, upon an honorable pare of Crowtches, from

hospitall to hospitall—fare ye well Sir. And yet do not you scorne
us, for places in the Court, are but [like] beds in the hospitall,
where this mans head lies at that mans foote, and so lower, and
lower.   *[exit*

DELIO. I knew this fellow (seaven yeares) in the Gallies,
For a notorious murther, and 'twas thought
The Cardinall suborn'd it: he was releas'd
By the French Generall (*Gaston de Foux*)
When he recover'd *Naples.*

ANTONIO. 'Tis great pitty
He should be thus neglected—I have heard
He's very valiant: This foule mellancholly
Will poyson all his goodnesse, for (i'le tell you)
If too immoderate sleepe be truly sayd
To be an inward rust unto the soule;
It then doth follow want of action
Breeds all blacke male-contents, and their close rearing
(Like mothes in cloath) doe hurt for want of wearing.

[*Enter Silvio, Castruchio, Roderigo, and Grisolan*]

DELIO. The Presence 'gins to fill, you promis'd me
To make me the partaker of the natures
Of some of your great Courtiers.

ANTONIO. The Lord Cardinall's
And other strangers', that are now in Court?—
I shall: here comes the great *Calabrian* Duke.   [*enter Ferdinand*

FERDINAND. Who tooke the Ring oftnest?

SILVIO. *Antoni*[o] *Bologna* (my Lord).

FERDINAND. Our Sister Duchesse' great Master of her house-
hold? Give him the Jewell: when shall we leave this sportive-
action, and fall to action indeed?

CASTRUCHIO. Me thinkes (my Lord) you should not desire to
go to war, in person.

FERDINAND. Now, for some gravity: why (my Lord?)

CASTRUCHIO. It is fitting a Souldier arise to be a Prince, but
not necessary a Prince descend to be a Captaine.

FERDINAND. Noe?

CASTRUCHIO. No, (my Lord) he were far better do it by a
Deputy.

FERDINAND. Why should he not as well sleepe, or eate, by a
Deputy? This might take idle, offensive, and base office from him,
whereas the other deprives him of honour.

CASTRUCHIO. Beleeve my experience: that Realme is never long in quiet, where the Ruler, is a Souldier.

FERDINAND. Thou toldst me thy wife could not endure fighting.

CASTRUCHIO. True (my Lord.)

F[ER]DINAND. And of a jest, she broke of a Captaine she met, full of wounds: I have forgot it.

CASTRUCHIO. She told him (my Lord) he was a pittifull fellow, to lie, like the Children of *Ismael*, all in Tents.

FERDINAND. Why, there's a wit were able to undoe all the Chyrurgeons o'the City, for although Gallants should quarrell, and had drawne their weapons, and were ready to goe to it; yet her perswasions would make them put up.

CASTRUCHIO. That she would (my Lord)—How doe you like my Spanish Gennit?

RODERIGO. He is all fire.

FERDINAND. I am of *Pliney's* opinion, I thinke he was begot by the wind, he runs, as if he were ballass'd with Quick-silver.

SILVIO. True (my Lord) he reeles from the Tilt often.

RODERIGO, GRISOLAN. Ha, ha, ha.

FERDINAND. Why do you laugh? Me thinks you that are Courtiers should be my touch-wood, take fire, when I give fire; that is, laugh when I laugh, were the subject never so wity—

CASTRUCHIO. True (my Lord) I my selfe have heard a very good jest, and have scorn'd to seeme to have so silly a wit, as to understand it.

FERDINAND. But I can laugh at your Foole (my Lord.)

CASTRUCHIO. He cannot speake (you know) but he makes faces, my lady cannot abide him.

FERDINAND. Noe?

CASTRUCHIO. Nor endure to be in merry Company: for she saies too much laughing, and too much Company, fils her too full of the wrinckle.

FERDINAND. I would then have a Mathematicall Instrument made for her face, that she might not laugh out of compasse: I shall shortly visit you at *Millaine* (Lord *Silvio*.)

SILVIO. Your Grace shall arrive most wel-come.

FERDINAND. You are a good Horse-man (*Antonio*) you have excellent Riders in *France*—what doe you thinke of good Horse-man-ship?

ANTONIO. Noblely (my Lord)—as out of the Grecian-horse, issued many famous Princes: So, out of brave Horse-man-ship, arise the first Sparkes of growing resolution, that raise the minde to noble action.

FERDINAND. You have be-spoake it worthely.

SILVIO. Your brother, the Lord Cardinall, and sister Dutchesse.

[enter Cardinal, Duchess, Cariola, and Julia

CARDINALL. Are the Gallies come about?

GRISOLAN. They are (my Lord.)

FERDINAND. Here's the Lord *Silvio*, is come to take his leave.

DELIO. Now (Sir) your promise: what's that Cardinall?
I meane his Temper? they say he's a brave fellow,
Will play his five thousand crownes, at Tennis, Daunce,
Court Ladies, and one that hath fought single Combats.

ANTONIO. Some such flashes superficially hang on him, for
forme: but observe his inward Character: he is a mellancholly
Churchman: The Spring in his face, is nothing but the Ingendring
of Toades: where he is jealious of any man, he laies worse plots for
them, then ever was impos'd on *Hercules*: for he strewes in his way
Flatter[er]s, Panders, Intelligencers, Athiests, and a thousand such
politicall Monsters: he should have beene Pope: but in stead of
comming to it by the primative decensie of the church, he did
bestow bribes, so largely, and so impudently, as if he would have
carried it away without heavens knowledge. Some good he hath
done.

DELIO. You have given too much of him: what's his brother?

ANTONIO. The Duke there? a most perverse, and turbulent
        Nature—
What appeares in him mirth, is meerely outside,
If he laugh hartely, it is to laugh
All honesty out of fashion.

DELIO. Twins?

ANTONIO. In qualitie:
He speakes with others Tongues, and heares mens suites,
With others Eares: will seeme to sleepe o'th bench
Onely to intrap offenders, in their answeres;
Doombes men to death, by information,
Rewards, by heare-say.

DELIO. Then the Law to him
Is like a fowle blacke cob-web, to a Spider—
He makes it his dwelling, and a prison
To entangle those shall feede him.

ANTONIO. Most true:
He nev'r paies debts, unlesse they be [shrewd] turnes,
And those he will confesse that he doth owe.
Last: for his brother, there, (the Cardinall)
They that doe flatter him most, say Oracles

Hang at his lippes: and verely I beleeve them:
For the Divell speakes in them.
But for their sister, (the right noble Duchesse)
You never fix'd you[r] eye on three faire Meddalls,
Cast in one figure, of so different temper:
For her discourse, it is so full of Rapture,
You onely will begin, then to be sorry
When she doth end her speech: and wish (in wonder)
She held it lesse vaine-glory, to talke much,
Then your pennance, to heare her: whilst she speakes,
She throwes upon a man so sweet a looke,
That it were able raise one to a Galliard
That lay in a dead palsey; and to doate
On that sweete countenance: but in that looke,
There speaketh so divine a continence,
As cuts off all lascivious, and vaine hope.
Her dayes are practis'd in such noble vertue,
That sure her nights (nay more her very Sleepes)
Are more in Heaven, then other Ladies Shrifts.
Let all sweet Ladies breake their flattring Glasses,
And dresse themselves in her.
   DELIO. Fye *Antoni[o]*,
You play the wire-drawer with her commendations.
   ANTONIO. I'll case the picture up: onely thus much—
All her particular worth growes to this somme:
She staines the time past: lights the time to come—
   CARIOLA. You must attend my Lady, in the gallery,
Some halfe an houre hence.
   ANTONIO. I shall.   *[exeunt Antonio and Delio*
   FERDINAND. Sister, I have a suit to you:
   DUCHESS. To me, Sir?
   FERDINAND. A Gentleman here: *Daniel de Bosola*:
One, that was in the Gallies.
   DUCHESS. Yes, I know him:
   FERDINAND. A worthy fellow h'is: pray let me entreat for
The provisorship of your horse.
   DUCHESS. Your knowledge of him,
Commends him, and prefers him.
   FERDINAND. Call him heither,   *[exit Servant*
Wee [are] now upon parting: Good Lord *Silvio*
Do us commend to all our noble friends
At the League[r].
   SILVIO. Sir, I shall.

[DUCHESS.] You are for *Millaine?*

SILVIO. I am:

DUCHESS. Bring the Carroches: we'll bring you down to the
Haven.   [*exeunt, except Cardinall and Ferdinand*

CARDINALL. Be sure you entertaine that *Bosola*
For your Intelligence: I would not be seene in't.
And therefore many times I have slighted him,
When he did court our furtherance: as this Morning.

FERDINAND. *Antonio*, the great Master of her houshold
Had beene farre fitter:

CARDINALL. You are deceiv'd in him,
His Nature is too honest for such businesse,
He comes: I'll leave you: [*exit, enter Bosola*

BOSOLA. I was lur'd to you.

FERDINAND. My brother here (the Cardinall) could never
abide you.

BOSOLA. Never since he was in my debt.

FERDINAND. May be some oblique character in your face,
Made him suspect you?

BOSOLA. Doth he study Phisiognomie?
There's no more credit to be given to th'face,
Then to a sicke mans uryn, which some call
The Physitians whore, because she cozens him:
He did suspect me wrongfully:

FERDINAND. For that
You must give great men leave to take their times:
Distrust, doth cause us seldome be deceiv'd;
You see, the oft shaking of the Cedar-Tree
Fastens it more at roote.

BOSOLA. Yet take heed:
For to suspect a friend unworthely,
Instructs him the next way to suspect you,
And prompts him to deceive you.

[F]ERDINAND. There's gold.

BOSOLA. So:
What followes? (Never raind such showres as these
Without thunderbolts i'th taile of them;) whose throat must
I cut?

FERDINAND. Your inclination to shed blood rides post
Before my occasion to use you: I give you that
To live i'th Court, here: and observe the Duchesse,
To note all the particulars of her haviour:
What suitors doe sollicite her for marriage

And whom she best affects: she's a yong widowe,
I would not have her marry againe.

    BOSOLA. No, Sir?

    FERDINAND. Doe not you aske the reason: but be satisfied,
I say I would not.

    BOSOLA. It seemes you would create me
One of your familiars.

    FERDINAND. Familiar? what's that?

    BOSOLA. Why, a very quaint invisible Divell, in flesh:
An Intelligencer.

    FERDINAND. Such a kind of thriving thing
I would wish thee: and ere long, thou maist arrive
At a higher place by't.

    BOSOLA. Take your Divels
Which Hell calls Angels: these curs'd gifts would make
You a corrupter, me an impudent traitor,
And should I take these, they'll'd take me [to] Hell.

    FERDINAND. Sir, I'll take nothing from you, that I have given:
There is a place, that I procur'd for you
This morning: (the Provisor-ship o'th' horse)—
Have you heard o[n']t?

    BOSOLA. Noe.

    FERDINAND. 'Tis yours, is't not worth thankes?

    BOSOLA. I would have you curse your selfe now, that your
        bounty
(Which makes men truly noble) ere should make
Me a villaine: oh, that to avoid ingratitude
For the good deed you have done me, I must doe
All the ill man can invent: Thus the Divell
Candies all sinnes [o'er]: and what Heaven termes vild,
That names he complementall.

    FERDINAND. Be your selfe:
Keepe your old garbe of melencholly: 'twill expresse
You envy those that stand above your reach,
Yet strive not to come neere'em: This will gaine
Accesse, to private lodgings, where your selfe
May (like a pollitique dormouse—

    BOSOLA. As I have seene some,
Feed in a Lords dish, halfe asleepe, not seeming
To listen to any talke: and yet these Rogues
Have cut his throat in a dreame: whats my place?
The Proviso[r]-ship o'th horse? say then my corruption
Grew out of horse-doong: I am your creature.

FERDINAND. Away!

BOSOLA. Let good men, for good deeds, covet good fame,
Since place, and riches oft are bribes of shame—
Sometimes the Divell doth preach.   [*exit Bosola*

[*enter Cardinal, Duchess, and Cariola*

CARDINALL. We are to part from you: and your owne dis-
cretion
Must now be your director.

FERDINAND. You are a Widowe:
You know already what man is: and therefore
Let not youth...high promotion, eloquence—

CARDINALL. No, nor any thing without the addition, *Honor*,
Sway your high blood.

FERDINAND. Marry? they are most luxurious,
Will wed twice.

CARDINALL. O fie!

FERDINAND. Their livers are more spotted
Then *Labans* sheepe.

DUCHESS. Diamonds are of most value
They say, that have past through most Jewellers hands.

FERDINAND. Whores, by that rule, are precious:

DUCHESS. Will you heare me?
I'll never marry:

CARDINALL. So most Widowes say:
But commonly that motion lasts no longer
Then the turning of an houreglasse—the funeral Sermon,
And it, end both together.

FERDINAND. Now heare me:
You live in a ranke pasture here, i'th Court—
There is a kind of honney-dew, that's deadly:
'Twill poyson your fame; looke [to]'t: be not cunning:
For they whose faces doe belye their hearts,
Are Witches, ere they arrive at twenty yeeres,
I: and give the divell sucke.

DUCHESS. This is terrible good councell:

FERDINAND. Hypocrisie is woven of a fine small thred,
Subtler, then *Vulcans* Engine: yet (beleev't)
Your darkest actions: nay, your privat'st thoughts,
Will come to light.

CARDINALL. You may flatter your selfe,
And take your owne choice: privately be married
Under the E[a]ves of night...

FERDINAND. Think't the best voyage
That ere you made; like the irregular Crab,
Which though't goes backward, thinkes that it goes right,
Because it goes its owne way: but observe;
Such weddings, may more properly be said
To be executed, then celibrated.
　　CARDINALL. The marriage night
Is the entrance into some prison.
　　FERDINAND. And those joyes,
Those lustfull pleasures, are like heavy sleepes
Which doe fore-run mans mischiefe.
　　CARDINALL. Fare you well.
Wisdome begins at the end: remember it.　　　　　　　　[exit
　　DUCHESS. I thinke this speech betweene you both was studied,
It came so roundly off.
　　FERDINAND. You are my sister,
This was my Fathers poyniard: doe you see,
I'll'd be loth to see't looke rusty, 'cause 'twas his:
I would have you to give ore these chargeable Revels;
A Vizor, and a Masque are whispering roomes
That were nev'r built for goodnesse: fare ye well:
And woemen like that part, which (like the Lamprey)
Hath nev'r a bone in't.
　　DUCHESS. Fye Sir!
　　FERDINAND. Nay,
I meane the Tongue: varietie of Courtship;
What cannot a neate knave with a smooth tale,
Make a woman beleeve? farewell, lusty Widowe.　　　[exit
　　DUCHESS. Shall this move me? if all my royall kindred
Lay in my way unto this marriage:
I'll'd make them my low foote-steps: And even now,
Even in this hate (as men in some great battailes
By apprehending danger, have atchiev'd
Almost impossible actions: I have heard Souldiers say so),
So I, through frights, and threatnings, will assay
This dangerous venture: Let old wives report
I wincked, and chose a husband: *Cariola*,
To thy knowne secricy, I have given up
More then my life, my fame:
　　CAR[IOL]A. Both shall be safe:
For I'll conceale this secret from the world
As warily as those that trade in poyson,
Keepe poyson from their children.

DUCHESS. Thy protestation
Is ingenious, and hearty: I beleeve it.
Is *Antonio* come?
  CARIOLA. He attends you:
  DUCHESS. Good deare soule,
Leave me: but place thy selfe behind the Arras,
Where thou maist over-heare us: wish me good speed   *[Cariola*
For I am going into a wildernesse,   *withdraws behind*
Where I shall find nor path, nor friendly clewe   *the arras:*
To be my guide—I sent for you, Sit downe: *the Duchess*
Take Pen and Incke, and write: are you ready?   *draws the*
  ANTONIO. Yes: *traverse*
  DUCHESS. What did I say?   *revealing Antonio*
  ANTONIO. That I should write some-what.
  DUCHESS. Oh, I remember:
After [these] triumphs, and this large expence
It's fit (like thrifty husbands) we enquire
What's laid up for to-morrow:
  ANTONIO. So please your beauteous Excellence.
  DUCHESS. Beauteous?
Indeed I thank you: I look yong for your sake.
You have tane my cares upon you.
  ANTONIO. I'le fetch your Grace
The particulars of your revinew, and expence.
  DUCHESS. Oh, you are an upright treasurer: but you mistooke,
For when I said I meant to make enquiry,
What's layd up for to-morrow: I did meane
What's layd up yonder for me.
  ANTONIO. Where?
  DUCHESS. In Heaven,
I am making my will, (as 'tis fit Princes should
In perfect memory) and I pray Sir, tell me
Were not one better make it smiling, thus?
Then in deepe groanes, and terrible ghastly lookes,
As if the guifts we parted with, procur'd
That violent distr[a]ction?
  ANTONIO. Oh, much better.
  DUCHESS. If I had a husband now, this care were quit:
But I intend to make yo[u] Over-seer;
What good deede, shall we first remember? say.
  ANTONIO. Begin with that first good deed began i'th'world,
After mans creation, the Sacrament of marriage—
I'ld have you first provide for a good husband,

Give him all.

DUCHESS. All?

ANTONIO. Yes, your excellent selfe.

DUCHESS. In a winding sheete?

ANTONIO. In a cople.

DUCHESS. St. *Win[i]frid*, that were a strange will.

ANTONIO. 'Twere strange
If there were no will in you to marry againe.

DUCHESS. What doe you thinke of marriage?

ANTONIO. I take't, as those that deny Purgatory,
It locally containes, or heaven, or hell,
There's no third place in't.

DUCHESS. How doe you affect it?

ANTONIO. My banishment, feeding my mellancholly,
Would often reason thus.

DUCHESS. Pray let's heare it.

ANTONIO. Say a man never marry, nor have children,
What takes that from him? onely the bare name
Of being a father, or the weake delight
To see the little wanton ride a cocke-horse
Upon a painted sticke, or heare him chatter
Like a taught Starling.

DUCHESS. Fye, fie, what's all this?
One of your eyes is blood-shot, use my Ring to't,
They say 'tis very soveraigne, 'twas my wedding Ring,
And I did vow never to part with it,
But to my second husband.

ANTONIO. You have parted with it now.

DUCHESS. Yes, to helpe your eye-sight.

ANTONIO. You have made me starke blind.

DUCHESS. How?

ANTONIO. There is a sawcy, and ambitious divell
Is dauncing in this circle.

DUCHESS. Remoove him.

ANTONIO. How?

DUCHESS. There needs small conjuration, when your finger
May doe it: thus, is it fit?

ANTONIO. What sayd you?   [*he kneeles*

DUCHESS. Sir,
This goodly roofe of yours, is too low built,
I cannot stand upright in't, nor discourse,
Without I raise it higher: raise your selfe,
Or if you please, my hand to helpe you: so.

ANTONIO. Ambition (Madam) is a great mans madnes,
That is not kept in chaines, and close-pent-roomes,
But in faire lightsome lodgings, and is girt
With the wild noyce of pratling visitan[t]s,
Which makes it lunatique, beyond all cure—
Conceive not, I am so stupid, but I ayme
Whereto your favours tend: But he's a foole
That (being a-cold) would thrust his hands i'th'fire
To warme them.

DUCHESS. So, now the ground's broake,
You may discover what a wealthy Mine,
I make you Lord [of].

ANTONIO. Oh my unworthinesse.

DUCHESS. You were ill to sell your selfe,
This darkning of your worth, is not like that
Which trades-men use i'th'City—their false lightes
Are to rid bad wares off: and I must tell you
If you will know where breathes a compleat man,
(I speake it without flattery) turne your eyes,
And progresse through your selfe.

ANTONIO. Were there nor heaven, nor hell,
I should be honest: I have long serv'd vertue,
And nev'r tane wages of her.

DUCHESS. Now she paies it—
The misery of us, that are borne great!—
We are forc'd to wo[o], because none dare wo[o] us:
And as a Tyrant doubles with his words,
And fearefully equivocates: so we
Are forc'd to expresse our violent passions
In ridles, and in dreames, and leave the path
Of simple vertue, which was never made
To seeme the thing it is not: Goe, go brag
You have left me heartlesse—mine is in your bosome,
I hope 'twill multiply love there: You doe tremble:
Make not your heart so dead a peece of flesh
To feare, more then to love me: Sir, be confident,
What is't distracts you? This is flesh, and blood, (Sir,)
'Tis not the figure cut in Allablaster
Kneeles at my husbands tombe: Awake, awake (man)
I do here put of[f] all vaine ceremony,
And onely doe appeare to you a yong widow
That claimes you for her husband, and like a widow,
I use but halfe a blush in't.

ANTONIO. Truth speake for me,
I will remaine the constant Sanctuary
Of your good name.
     DUCHESS. I thanke you (gentle love)
And 'cause you shall not come to me in debt,
(Being now my Steward) here upon your lippes
I signe your *Quietus est*: This you should have beg'd now,
I have seene children oft eate sweete-meates thus,
As fearefull to devoure them too soone.
     ANTONIO. But for your Brothers?
     DUCHESS. Do not thinke of them,
All discord, without this circumference,   [*she puts her arms*
Is onely to be pittied, and not fear'd: *about him*
Yet, should they know it, time will easily
Scatter the tempest.
     ANTONIO. These words should be mine,
And all the parts you have spoke, if some part of it
Would not have savour'd flattery.
     DUCHESS. Kneele.   [*Cariola shows herself*
     ANTONIO. Hah?
     DUCHESS. Be not amaz'd, this woman's of my Councell,
I have heard Lawyers say, a contract in a Chamber,
(*Per verba [de] presenti*) is absolute marriage:
Blesse (Heaven) this sacred Gordian, which let violence
Never untwine.
     ANTONIO. And may our sweet affections, (like the Sphears)
Be still in motion.
     DUCHESS. Quickning, and make
The like soft Musique.
     ANTONIO. That we may imitate the loving Palmes
(Best Embleme of a peacefull marriage)
That nev'r bore fruite devided.
     DUCHESS. What can the Church force more?
     ANTONIO. That Fortune may not know an accident
Either of joy, or sorrow, to devide
Our fixed wishes.
     DUCHESS. How can the Church build faster?
We now are man, and wife, and 'tis the Church
That must but eccho this: Maid, stand apart,
I now am blinde.
     ANTONIO. What's your conceit in this?
     DUCHESS. I would have you leade your Fortune by the hand,
Unto your marriage bed:

(You speake in me this, for we now are one)
We'll onely lie, and talke together, and plot
T'appease my humorous kindred; and if you please
(Like the old tale, in *Alexander* and *Lodowicke*)
Lay a naked sword betweene us, keepe us chast:
Oh, let me shrowd my blushes in your bosome,
Since 'tis the treasury of all my secrets.

   CARIOLA.   Whether the spirit of greatnes, or of woman
Raigne most in her, I know not, but it shewes
A fearefull madnes. I owe her much of pitty.   [*exeunt*

Castruchio

ACTUS II. SCENA I

[The Same]

[Enter Bosola and Castruchio]

BOSOLA. You say you would faine be taken—for an eminent Courtier?

CASTRUCHIO. 'Tis the very maine of my ambition.

BOSOLA. Let me see, you have a reasonable good face for't already, and your night-cap expresses your eares sufficient largely —I would have you learne to twirle the strings of your band with a good grace; and in a set speech, (at th'end of every sentence,) to hum, three, or foure times, or blow your nose (till it smart againe,) to recover your memory—when you come to be a president in criminall causes, if you smile upon a prisoner, hang him, but if you frowne upon him, and threaten him, let him be sure to scape the Gallowes.

CASTRUCHIO. I would be a very merrie president—

BOSOLA. Do not sup a nights, 'twill beget you an admirable wit.

CASTRUCHIO. Rather it would make me have a good stomake to quarrel, for they say, your roaring-boyes eate meate seldome, and that makes them so valiant: but how shall I know whether the people take me for an eminent fellow?

BOSOLA. I will teach a tricke to know it—give out you lie a-dying, and if you heare the common people curse you, be sure you

are taken for one of the prime night-caps—[*enter Old Lady*] You
come from painting now?

OLD LADY. From what?

BOSOLA. Why, from your scurvy face-physicke—to behold thee
not painted enclines somewhat neere a miracle: These…in thy
face here, were deepe rutts, and foule sloughes the last progresse:
There was a Lady in *France*, that having had the small pockes,
flead the skinne off her face, to make it more levell; and whereas
before she look'd like a Nutmeg-grater, after she resembled an
abortive hedge-hog.

OLD LADY. Do you call this painting?

BOSOLA. No, no, but [I] call [it] carreening of an old mor-
phew'd Lady, to make her disembogue againe—There's rough-cast
phrase to your plastique.

OLD LADY. It seemes you are well acquainted with my closset?

BOSOLA. One would suspect it for a shop of witch-craft, to finde
in it the fat of Serpents; spawne of Snakes, Jewes spittle, and their
yong children['s] ordures—and all these for the face: I would
sooner eate a dead pidgeon, taken from the soles of the feete of one
sicke of the plague, then kisse one of you fasting: here are two of
you, whose sin of your youth is the very patrimony of the Physition,
makes him renew his foote-cloth with the Spring, and change his
high-priz'd curtezan with the fall of the leafe: I do wonder you doe
not loath your selves—observe my meditation now:
What thing is in this outward forme of man
To be belov'd? we account it ominous,
If Nature doe produce a Colt, or Lambe,
A Fawne, or Goate, in any limbe resembling
A Man; and flye from't as a prodegy.
Man stands amaz'd to see his deformity,
In any other Creature but himselfe.
But in our owne flesh, though we beare diseases
Which have their true names onely tane from beasts,
As the most ulcerous Woolfe, and swinish Meazeall;
Though we are eaten up of lice, and wormes,
And though continually we beare about us
A rotten and dead body, we delight
To hide it in rich tissew—all our feare,
(Nay all our terrour) is, least our Phisition
Should put us in the ground, to be made sweete.
Your wife's gone to *Rome*: you two cople, and get you
To the wels at *Leuca*, to recover your aches.   [*exeunt Castruchio
I have other worke on foote: I observe our Duchesse   *and Old Lady*

Is sicke a dayes, she puykes, her stomacke seethes,
The fins of her eie-lids looke most teeming blew,
She waines i'th'cheeke, and waxes fat i'th'flanke;
And (contrary to our *Italian* fashion,)
Weares a loose-bodied Gowne—there's somewhat in't,
I have a tricke, may chance discover it
(A pretty one)—I have bought some Apricocks,
The first our Spring yeelds.   [*enter Delio and Antonio*

    DELIO. And so long since married?
You amaze me.

    ANTONIO. Let me seale your lipps for ever,
For did I thinke, that any thing but th'ayre
Could carry these words from you, I should wish
You had no breath at all: [*to Bosola*] Now Sir, in your contemplation?
You are studdying to become a great wise fellow?

    BOSOLA. Oh Sir, the opinion of wisedome is a foule tettor, that
runs all over a mans body: if simplicity direct us to have no evill,
it directs us to a happy being: For the subtlest folly proceedes
from the subtlest wisedome: Let me be simply honest.

    ANTONIO. I do understand your in-side.

    BOSOLA. Do you so?

    ANTONIO. Because you would not seeme to appeare to th'world
Puff'd up with your preferment: You continue
This out of [f]ashion mellancholly—leave it, leave it.

    BOSOLA. Give me leave to be honest in any phrase, in any
complement whatsoever—shall I confesse my selfe to you? I looke
no higher then I can reach: they are the gods, that must ride on
winged horses, a Lawyers mule of a slow pace will both suit my
disposition, and businesse: For (marke me) when a mans mind
rides faster then his horse can gallop, they quickly both tyre.

    ANTONIO. You would looke up to Heaven, but I thinke
The Divell, that rules i'th'aire, stands in your light.

    BOSOLA. Oh (Sir) you are Lord of the ascendant, chiefe man
with the Duchesse, a Duke was your cosen German, remov'd: Say
you were lineally descended from King *Pippin*, or he himselfe,
what of this? search the heads of the greatest rivers in the World,
you shall finde them but bubles of water: Some would thinke the
soules of Princes were brought forth by some more weighty cause,
then those of meaner persons—they are deceiv'd, there's the same
hand to them: The like passions sway them, the same reason, that
makes a Vicar goe to Law for a tithe-pig, and undoe his neigh-
bours, makes them spoile a whole Province, and batter downe
goodly Cities, with the Cannon.   [*enter Duchess and Ladies*

DUCHESS. Your arme *Antonio*, do I not grow fat?
I am exceeding short-winded: *Bosola,*
I would have you (Sir) provide for me a Littor,
Such a one, as the Duchesse of *Florence* roade in.

BOSOLA. The Duchesse us'd one, when she was great with childe.

DUCHESS. I thinke she did: come hether, mend my ruffe—
Here, when? thou art such a tedious Lady; and
Thy breath smells of Lymmon pils, would thou hadst done—
Shall I sound under thy fingers? I am so troubled
With the mother.

BOSOLA. [*aside*] I feare to[o] much.

DUCHESS. I have heard you say, that the French Courtie[r]s
Weare their hats on fore the King.

ANTONIO. I have seene it.

DUCHESS. In the Presence?

ANTONIO. Yes:

[DUCHESS.] Why should not we bring up that fashion?
'Tis ceremony more then duty, that consists
In the remooving of a peece of felt:
Be you the example to the rest o'th' Court,
Put on your hat first.

ANTONIO. You must pardon me:
I have seene, in colder countries then in *France,*
Nobles stand bare to th'Prince; and the distinction
M[e]thought show'd reverently.

BOSOLA. I have a present for your Grace.

DUCHESS. For me sir?

BOSOLA. Apricocks (Madam.)

DUCHESS. O sir, where are they?
I have heard of none to yeare.

BOSOLA. [*aside*] Good, her colour rises.

DUCHESS. Indeed I thanke you: they are wondrous faire ones:
What an unskilfull fellow is our Gardiner!
We shall have none this moneth.

BOSOLA. Will not your Grace pare them?

DUCHESS. No, they tast of muske (me thinkes) indeed they doe:

BOSOLA. I know not: yet I wish your Grace had parde 'em:

DUCHESS. Why?

BOSOLA. I forgot to tell you the knave Gardner,
(Onely to raise his profit by them the sooner)
Did ripen them in horse-doung.

DUCHESS. O you jest:
You shall judge: pray tast one.

ANTONIO. Indeed Madam,
I doe not love the fruit.
DUCHESS. Sir, you are loath
To rob us of our dainties: 'tis a delicate fruit,
They say they are restorative?
BOSOLA. 'Tis a pretty
Art: this grafting.
DUCHESS. 'Tis so: a bettring of nature.
BOSOLA. To make a pippin grow upon a crab,
A dampson on a black thorne: [*aside*] how greedily she eats them!
A whirlewinde strike off these bawd-farthingalls,
For, but for that, and the loose-bodied gowne,
I should have discover'd apparently
The young spring-hall cutting a caper in her belly.
DUCHESS. I thanke you (*Bosola*:) they were right good ones,
If they doe not make me sicke.
ANTONIO. How now Madame?
DUCHESS. This greene fruit...and my stomake are not friends—
How they swell me!
BOSOLA. [*aside*] Nay, you are too much swell'd already.
DUCHESS. Oh, I am in an extreame cold sweat.
BOSOLA. I am very sorry: [*exit*
DUCHESS. Lights to my chamber: O, good *Antonio*,
I feare I am undone.   [*exit Duchesse*
DELIO. Lights there, lights!
ANTONIO. O my most trusty *Delio*, we are lost:
I feare she's falne in labour: and ther's left
No time for her remove.
DELIO. Have you prepar'd
Those Ladies to attend her? and procur'd
That politique safe conveyance for the Mid-wife
Your Duchesse plotted?
ANTONIO. I have:
DELIO. Make use then of this forc'd occasion:
Give out that *Bosola* hath poyson'd her,
With these Apricocks: that will give some colour
For her keeping close.
ANTONIO. Fye, fie, the Physitians
Will then flocke to her.
DELIO. For that you may pretend
She'll use some prepar'd Antidote of her owne,
Least the Physitians should repoyson her.
ANTONIO. I am lost in amazement: I know not what to think
      on't.   [*exeunt*

SCENA II

[The Same]

[Enter Bosola and Old Lady]

BOSOLA. *[aside]* So, so: ther's no question but her teatchi[n]es and most vulterous eating of the Apricocks, are apparant signes of breeding—*[to the Old Lady]* now?

OLD LADY. I am in hast (Sir.)

BOSOLA. There was a young wayting-woman, had a monstrous desire to see the Glasse-house.

OLD LADY. Nay, pray let me goe:

BOSOLA. And it was onely to know what strange instrument it was, should swell up a glasse to the fashion of a womans belly.

OLD LADY. I will heare no more of the Glasse-house—you are still abusing woemen?

BOSOLA. Who—I? no, onely (by the way now and then) mention your fraileties. The Orrenge tree bear[s] ripe and greene fruit, and blossoms altogether: And some of you give entertainment for pure love: but more, for more precious reward. The lusty Spring smels well: but drooping Autumne tasts well: If we have the same golden showres, that rained in the time of *Jupiter* the Thunderer: you have the same *Dan[a]es* still, to hold up their laps to receive them: didst thou never study the *Mathematiques?*

OLD LADY. What's that (Sir?)

BOSOLA. Why, to know the trick how to make a many lines meete in one center: Goe, goe; give your foster-daughters good councell: tell them, that the Divell takes delight to hang at a womans girdle, like a false rusty watch, that she cannot discerne how the time passes.   *[exit Old Lady: enter Antonio, Delio,*

ANTONIO. Shut up the Court gates: *Roderigo, and Grisolan*

RODERIGO. Why sir? what's the danger?

ANTONIO. Shut up the Posternes presently: and call All the Officers o'th' Court.

GRISOLAN. I shall instantly: *[exit*

ANTONIO. Who keepes the key o'th' Parke-gate?

RODERIGO. *Forobosco.*

ANTONIO. Let him bring't presently.

                              [re-enter Grisolan with Servants

SERVANT. Oh, Gentlemen o'th' Court, the fowlest treason.

BOSOLA. *[aside]* If that these Apricocks should be poysond, now; Without my knowledge!

SERVANT. There was taken even now
A Switzer in the Duchesse Bed-chamber.
2. SERVANT. A Switzer?
SERVANT. With a Pistoll in his great cod-piece.
BOSOLA. H[a], ha, ha.
SERVANT. The cod-piece was the case for't.
2. SERVANT. There was a cunning traitor.
Who would have search'd his cod-piece?
SERVANT. True, if he had kept out of the Ladies chambers:
And all the mowldes of his buttons, were leaden bullets.
2. SERVANT. Oh wicked Caniball: a fire-lock in's cod-piece?
SERVANT. 'Twas a French plot, upon my life.
2. SERVANT. To see what the Divell can doe!
ANTONIO. All the Office[r]s here?
SERVANTS. We are:
ANTONIO. Gentlemen,
We have lost much Plate you know; and but this evening
Jewels, to the value of foure thousand Duckets
Are missing in the Du[tc]hesse Cabinet—
Are the Gates shut?
SERVANT. Yes.
ANTONIO. 'Tis the Duchesse pleasure
Each Officer be lock'd into his chamber
Till the Sun-rysing: and to send the keyes
Of all their chests, and of their outward doores
Into her bed-chamber: She is very sicke.
RODERIGO. At her pleasure.
ANTONIO. She intreates you take't not ill: The Innocent
Shall be the more approv'd by it.
BOSOLA. Gentleman o'th' Wood-yard, where's your Switzer
   now?
SERVANT. By this hand, 'twas creadably reported by one o'th'
   Black-guard.   [exeunt except Antonio and Delio
DELIO. How fares it with the Dutchesse?
ANTONIO. She's expos'd
Unto the worst of torture, paine, and feare;
DELIO. Speake to her all happy comfort.
ANTONIO. How I do play the foole with mine own danger!
You are this night (deere friend) to poast to Rome,
My life lies in your service.
DELIO. Doe not doubt me—
ANTONIO. Oh, 'Tis farre from me: and yet feare presents me
Somewhat that look[s] like danger.

DELIO. Beleeve it,
'Tis but the shadow of your feare, no more:
How superstitiously we mind our evils!
The throwing downe salt, or crossing of a Hare;
Bleeding at nose, the stumbling of a horse:
Or singing of a Criket, are of powre
To daunt whole man in us: Sir, fare you well:
I wish you all the joyes of a bless'd Father;
And (for my faith) lay this unto your brest,
Old friends (like old swords) still are trusted best.   [exit: enter
   CARIOLA. Sir, you are the happy father of a sonne,   Cariola
Your wife commends him to you.   with a child
   ANTONIO. Blessed comfort:
For heaven-sake tend her well: I'll presently
Goe set a figure for's Nativitie.   [exeunt

SCENA III

[*The Same. Outside the Palace*]

[*Enter Bosola, with a dark lanthorn*]

BOSOLA. Sure I did heare a woman shreike: list, hah!
And the sound came (if I receiv'd it right)
From the Dutchesse lodgings: ther's some stratagem
In the confyning all our Courtiers
To their severall wards: I must have part of it,
My Intelligence will freize else: List againe—
It may be 'twas the mellencholly bird,
(Best friend of silence, and of solitarines)
The Oowle, that scream'd so: hah? *Antonio?*
                    [*enter Antonio with a candle, his sword drawn*
   ANTONIO. I heard some noyse: [who's] there? what art thou?
      speake.
   BOSOLA. *Antonio?* Put not your face; nor body
To such a forc'd expression of feare—
I am *Bosola*; your friend.
   ANTONIO. *Bosola?*
(This Moale do's undermine me) heard you not
A noyce even now?
   BOSOLA. From whence?
   ANTONIO. From the *Duchesse* lodging.
   BOSOLA. Not I: did you?

ANTONIO. I did: or else I dream'd.

BOSOLA. Let's walke towards it.

ANTONIO. No: It may be, 'twas
But the rising of the winde:

BOSOLA. Very likely:
Me thinkes 'tis very cold, and yet you sweat.
You looke wildly.

ANTONIO. I have bin setting a figure
For the Dutchesse Jewells;

BOSOLA. Ah: and how falls your question?
Doe you find it radicall?

ANTONIO. What's that to you?
'Tis rather to be question'd what designe
(When all men were commanded to their lodgings)
Makes you a night-walker.

BOSOLA. In sooth I'll tell you:
Now all the Court's asleepe, I thought the Divell
Had least to doe here; I came to say my prayers,
And if it doe offend you I doe so,
You are a fine Courtier.

ANTONIO. [aside] This fellow will undoe me;
You gave the Dutchesse Apricocks to-day,
Pray heaven they werc not poysond?

BOSOLA. Poysond? a spanish figge
For the imputation.

ANTONIO. Traitors are ever confident,
Till they are discover'd: There were Jewels stolne too—
In my conceit, none are to be suspected
More then your selfe.

BOSOLA. You are a false steward.

ANTONIO. Sawcy slave! I'll pull thee up by the rootes;

BOSOLA. May be the ruyne will crush you to peeces.

ANTONIO. You are an impudent snake indeed (sir)—
Are you scarce warme, and doe you shew your sting?

[BOSOLA.]   .   .   .   .

ANTONIO. You Libell well (sir.)

BOSOLA. No (sir,) copy it out:
And I will set my hand to't.

ANTONIO. My nose bleedes:
One that were superstitious, would count
This ominous: when it meerely comes by chance.
Two letters, that are wrought here, for my name
Are drown'd in blood:

Meere accident: for you (sir) I'll take order:
I'th morne you shall be safe: [*aside*] 'tis that must colour
Her lying-in: sir, this doore you passe not:
I doe not hold it fit, that you come neere
The Dutchesse lodgings, till you have [quit] your selfe;
[*aside*] *The Great are like the Base; nay, they are the same,*
When they seeke shamefull waies, to avoid shame.   [*exit*

   BOSOLA. *Antonio* here about, did drop a Paper—
Some of your helpe (falce-friend)—oh, here it is:
What's here? a childes Nativitie calculated!

    The Dutchesse was deliver'd of a Sonne, 'tweene the houres
twelve, and one, in the night: Anno Dom: 1504. (*that's this yeere*)
decimo nono Decembris, (*that's this night*) *taken according to the*
Meridian of Malfy (*that's our Dutchesse: happy discovery!*). *The*
Lord of the first house, being combust in the ascendant, signifies short
life: and Mars *being in a human signe, joyn'd to the taile of the*
Dragon, in the eight house, doth threaten a violent death; Cæte[r]a
non scrutantur.

Why now 'tis most apparant: This precise fellow
Is the Dutchesse Bawde: I have it to my wish:
This is a parcell of Intelligency
Our Courtiers were [cas'de-up] for? It needes must follow,
That I must be committed, on pretence
Of poysoning her: which I'll endure, and laugh at:
If one could find the father now! but that
Time will discover; Old *Castruchio*
I'th morning poasts to Rome; by him I'll send
A Letter, that shall make her brothers Galls
Ore-flowe their Livours—this was a thrifty way.
   Though Lust doe masque in ne['e]r so strange disguise,
   She's oft found witty, but is never wise.   [*exit*

SCENA IIII

[*Rome. The Cardinal's Palace*]

[*Enter Cardinal and Julia*]

   CARDINALL. Sit: thou art my best of wishes—pre-thee tell me
What tricke didst thou invent to come to Rome,
Without thy husband?
   JULIA. Why, (my Lord) I told him
I came to visit an old Anchorite
Heare, for devotion.

CARDINALL. Thou art a witty false one:
I meane to him.
    JULIA. You have prevailed with me
Beyond my strongest thoughts: I would not now
Find you inconstant.
    CARDINALL. Doe not put thy selfe
To such a voluntary torture: which proceedes
Out of your owne guilt.
    JULIA. How (my Lord?)
    CARDINALL. You feare
My constancy, because you have approov'd
Those giddy and wild turning[s] in your selfe.
    JULIA. Did you ere find them?
    CARDINALL. Sooth generally for woemen,
A man might strive to make glasse male-able,
Ere he should make them fixed.
    JULIA. So, (my Lord)!—
    CARDINALL. We had need goe borrow that fantastique
        glasse
Invented by *Galileo* the Florentine,
To view another spacious world i'th' Moone,
And looke to find a constant woman there.
    JULIA. This is very well (my Lord.)
    CARDINALL. Why do you weepe?
Are teares your justification? the selfe-same teares
Will fall into your husbands bosome, (Lady)
With a loud protestation, that you love him
Above the world: Come, I'll love you wisely,
That's jealously, since I am very certaine
You cannot me make cuckould.
    JULIA. I'll go home
To my husband.
    CARDINALL. You may thanke me, (Lady)
I have taken you off your mellancholly pearch,
Boare you upon my fist, and shew'd you game,
And let you flie at it: I pray the[e] kisse me—
When thou wast with thy husband, thou wast watch'd
Like a tame Ellephant: (still you are to thanke me)
Thou hadst onely kisses from him, and high feeding,
But what delight was that? 'twas just like one
That hath a little fingring on the Lute,
Yet cannot tune it: (still you are to thanke me.)
    JULIA. You told me of a piteous wound i'th'heart,

And a sicke livour, when you woed me first,
And spake like one in physicke.
  CARDINALL. Who's that?   *[enter Servant*
Rest firme, for my affection to thee,
Lightning mooves slow to't.
  SERVANT. (Madam) a Gentleman
That's come post from *Malfy*, desires to see you.
  CARDINALL. Let him enter, I'll with-draw.   *[exit*
  SERVANT. He sayes,
Your husband (old *Castruchio*) is come to *Rome*,.
Most pittifully tyr'd with riding post.   *[exit: enter Delio*
  JULIA. Signior *Delio?* 'tis one of my old Suitors.
  DELIO. I was bold to come and see you.
  JULIA. Sir, [you] are wel-come.
  DELIO. Do you lie here?
  JULIA. Sure, your owne experience
Will satisfie you no—our Romane Prelates
Do not keepe lodging, for Ladies.
  DELIO. Very well:
I have brought you no comendations from your husband,
For I know none by him.
  JULIA. I heare he's come to *Rome*?
  DELIO. I never knew man, and beast, of a horse, and a
    knight,
So weary of each other—if he had had a good backe,
He would have undertooke to have borne his horse,
His breech was so pittifully sore.
  JULIA. Your laughter,
Is my pitty.
  DELIO. Lady, I know not whether
You want mony, but I have brought you some.
  JULIA. From my husband?
  DELIO. No, from mine owne allowance.
  JULIA. I must heare the condition, ere I be bound to take it.
  DELIO. Looke on't, 'tis gold, hath it not a fine colour?
  JULIA. I have a Bird more beautifull.
  DELIO. Try the sound on't.
  JULIA. A Lute-string far exceedes it,
It hath no smell, like Cassia, or Cyvit,
Nor is it phisicall, though some fond Doctors
Perswade us seeth'[t] in Cullisses—I'le tell you,
This is a Creature bred by——   *[enter Servant*
  SERVANT. Your husband's come,

Hath deliver'd a letter to the Duke of *Calabria*,
That, to my thinking hath put him out of his wits.   [*exit*
   JULIA. Sir, you heare,
'Pray let me know your busines, and your suite,
As briefely as can be.
   DELIO. With good speed, I would wish you
(At such time, as you are non-resident
With your husband) my mistris.
   JULIA. Sir, I'le go aske my husband if I shall,
And straight returne your answere.   [*exit*
   DELIO. Very fine—
Is this her wit, or honesty that speakes thus?
I heard one say the Duke was highly mov'd
With a letter sent from *Malfy*: I doe feare
Antonio is betray'd: how fearefully
Shewes his ambition now, (unfortunate Fortune)!—
"They passe through whirle-pooles, and deepe woes doe shun,
Who the event weigh, ere the action's done.   [*exit*

SCENA V

[*The Same*]

[*Enter*] *Cardinall, and Ferdinand, with a letter*

   FERDINAND. I have this night dig'd up a man-drake.
   CARDINALL. Say you?
   FERDINAND. And I am growne mad with't.
   CARDINALL. What's the pro[deg]y?
   FERDINAND. Read there—a sister dampn'd—she's loose
     i'th'hilts:
Growne a notorious Strumpet.
   CARDINALL. Speake lower.
   FERDINAND. Lower?
Rogues do not whisper't now, but seeke to publish't,
(As servants do the bounty of their Lords)
Aloud; and with a covetuous searching eye,
To marke who note them: Oh confusion sease her,
She hath had most cunning baudes to serve her turne,
And more secure conveyances for lust,
Then Townes of garrison, for Service.

CARDINALL. Is't possible?
Can this be certaine?
FERDINAND. Rubarbe, oh, for rubarbe
To purge this choller—here's the cursed day
To prompt my memory, and here'it shall sticke
Till of her bleeding heart, I make a spunge
To wipe it out.
CARDINALL. Why doe you make your selfe
So wild a Tempest?
FERDINAND. Would I could be one,
That I might tosse her pallace 'bout her eares,
Roote up her goodly forrests, blast her meades,
And lay her generall territory as wast,
As she hath done her honors.
CARDINALL. Shall our blood
(The royall blood of *Arragon*, and *Castile*)
Be thus attaincted?
FERDINAND. Apply desperate physicke—
We must not now use Balsamum, but fire,
The smarting cupping-glasse, for that's the meane
To purge infected blood, (such blood as hers:)
There is a kind of pitty in mine eie,
I'll give it to my hand-kercher; and now 'tis here,
I'll bequeath this to her Bastard.
CARDINALL. What to do?
FERDINAND. Why, to make soft lint for his mother['s]
        wounds,
When I have hewed her to peeces.
CARDINALL. Curs'd creature—
Unequall nature, to place womens hearts
So farre upon the left-side!
FERDINAND. Foolish men,
That ere will trust their honour in a Barke,
Made of so slight, weake bull-rush, as is woman,
Apt every minnit to sinke it!
CARDINALL. Thus Ignorance, when it hath purchas'd
        honour,
It cannot weild it.
FERDINAND. Me thinkes I see her laughing,
Excellent *Hyenna*—talke to me somewhat, quickly,
Or my imagination will carry me
To see her, in the shamefull act of sinne.
CARDINALL. With whom?

FERDINAND. Happily, with some strong-thigh'd Bargeman;
Or one [o']th'wood-yard, that can quoit the sledge,
Or tosse the barre, or else some lovely Squire
That carries coles up, to her privy lodgings.

    CARDINALL. You flie beyond your reason.

    FERDINAND. Goe to (Mistris.)
'Tis not your whores milke, that shall quench my wild-fire,
But your whores blood.

    CARDINALL. How idlely shewes this rage!—which carries
        you,
As men convai'd by witches, through the ayre,
On violent whirle-windes—this intemperate noyce,
Fitly resembles deafe-mens shrill discourse,
Who talke aloud, thinking all other men
To have their imperfection.

    FERDINAND. Have not you,
My palsey?

    CARDINALL. Yes—I can be angry
Without this rupture—there is not in nature
A thing, that makes man so deform'd, so beastly,
As doth intemperate anger: chide your selfe—
You have divers men, who never yet exprest
Their strong desire of rest, but by unrest,
By vexing of themselves: Come, put your selfe
In tune.

    FERDINAND. So—I will onely study to seeme
The thing I am not: I could kill her now,
In you, or in my selfe, for I do thinke
It is some sinne in us, Heaven doth revenge
By her.

    CARDINALL. Are you starke mad?

    FERDINAND. I would have their bodies
Burn't in a coale-pit, with the ventage stop'd,
That their curs'd smoake might not ascend to Heaven:
Or dippe the sheetes they lie in, in pitch or sulphure,
Wrap them in't, and then light them like a match:
Or else to boile their Bastard to a cullisse,
And give't his leacherous father, to renew
The sinne of his backe.

    CARDINALL. I'll leave you.

    FERDINAND. Nay, I have done,
I am confident, had I bin damn'd in hell,
And should have heard of this, it would have put me

Into a cold sweat: In, in, I'll go sleepe—
Till I know who leapes my sister, i'll not stirre:
That knowne, i'll finde Scorpions to string my whips,
And fix her in a generall ecclipse.   [*exeunt*

ACTUS III. SCENA I

[Amalfi. The Palace of the Duchess]

[Enter Antonio and Delio]

ANTONIO. Our noble friend (my most beloved *Delio*)
Oh, you have bin a stranger long at Court,
Came you along with the Lord *Ferdinand*?

DELIO. I did Sir, and how faires your noble *Duchesse*?

ANTONIO. Right fortunately well: She's an excellent
Feeder of pedegrees: since you last saw her,
She hath had two children more, a sonne, and daughter.

DELIO. Me thinkes 'twas yester-day: Let me but wincke,
And not behold your face, which to mine eye
Is somewhat leaner, verily I should dreame
It were within this halfe houre.

ANTONIO. You have not bin in Law, (friend *Delio*)
Nor in prison, nor a Suitor at the Court
Nor beg'd the reversion of some great mans place,
Nor troubled with an old wife, which doth make
Your time so inse[n]cibly hasten.

DELIO. 'Pray Sir tell me,
Hath not this newes arriv'd yet to the eare;
Of the Lord *Cardinall*?

ANTONIO. I feare it hath,
The Lord *Ferdinand*, (that's newly come to Court,)
Doth beare himselfe right dangerously.

DELIO. Pray why?

ANTONIO. He is so quiet, that he seemes to sleepe
The tempest out (as Dormise do in Winter)—
Those houses, that are haunted, are most still,
Till the divell be up.

DELIO. What say the common people?

ANTONIO. The common-rable, do directly say
She is a Strumpet.

DELIO. And your graver heades,
(Which would [b]e pollitique) what censure they?

ANTONIO. They do observe, I grow to infinite purchase
The leaft-hand way, and all suppose the Duchesse
Would amend it, if she could: For, say they,
Great Princes, though they grudge their Officers
Should have such large, and unconfined meanes
To get wealth under them, will not complaine
Least thereby they should make them odious
Unto the people—for other obligation
Of love, or marriage, betweene her and me,
They never dreame [of].   [enter Ferdinand, Duchess and Bosola

DELIO. The Lord Ferdinand
Is going to bed.

FERDINAND. I'll instantly to bed,
For I am weary: I am to be-speake
A husband for you.

DUCHESS. For me (Sir?)—'pray who is't?

FERDINAND. The great Count Malateste.

DUCHESS. Fie upon him,
A Count! he's a meere sticke of sugar-candy,
(You may looke quite thorough him)—when I choose
A husband, I will marry for your honour.

FERDINAND. You shall do well in't: How is't (worthy Antonio?)

DUCHESS. But (Sir) I am to have private conference with you,
About a scandalous report, is spread
Touching mine honour.

FERDINAND. Let me be ever deafe to't:
One of Pasquils paper-bullets, court calumney,
A pestilent ayre, which Princes pallaces
Are seldome purg'd [of]: Yet, say that it were true,
I powre it in your bosome, my fix'd love
Would strongly excuse, extenuate, nay deny
Faults, [were] they apparant in you: Goe be safe
In your owne innocency.

DUCHESS. [*aside*] Oh bless'd comfort—
This deadly aire is purg'd.   [*exeunt, except Ferdinand and Bosola*
 FERDINAND. Her guilt treads on
Hot burning cultures: Now *Bosola*,
How thrives our intelligence?
 BOSOLA. (Sir) uncertainly—
'Tis rumour'd she hath had three bastards, but
By whom, we may go read i'th' Starres.
 FERDINAND. Why some
Hold opinion, all things are written there.
 BOSOLA. Yes, if we could find Spectacles to read them—
I do suspect, there hath bin some Sorcery
Us'd on the Duchesse.
 FERDINAND. Sorcery?—to what purpose?
 BOSOLA. To make her doate on some desertles fellow,
She shames to acknowledge.
 FERDINAND. Can your faith give way
To thinke there's powre in potions, or in Charmes,
To make us love, whether we will or no?
 BOSOLA. Most certainely.
 FERDINAND. Away, these are meere gulleries, horred things
Invented by some cheating mounte-banckes
To abuse us: Do you thinke that hearbes, or charmes
Can force the will? Some trialls have bin made
In this foolish practise; but the ingredients
Were lenative poysons, such as are of force
To make the patient mad; and straight the witch
Sweares (by equivocation) they are in love.
The witch-craft lies in her rancke b[l]ood: this night
I will force confession from her: You told me
You had got (within these two dayes) a false key
Into her Bed-chamber.
 BOSOLA. I have.
 FERDINAND. As I would wish.
 BOSOLA. What doe you intend to doe?
 FERDINAND. Can you ghesse?
 BOSOLA. No:
 FERDINAND. Doe not aske then:
He that can compasse me, and know my drifts,
May say he hath put a girdle 'bout the world,
And sounded all her quick-sands.
 BOSOLA. I doe not
Thinke so.

FERDINAND. What doe you thinke then, pray?

BOSOLA. That you
Are your owne Chronicle too much: and grosly
Flatter your selfe.

FERDINAND. Give me thy hand, I thanke thee:
I never gave Pention but to flatterers,
Till I entertained thee: farewell,
That Friend a Great mans ruine strongely checks,
Who railes into his beliefe, all his defects.   [*exeunt*

SCENA II

[*The Bed-chamber of the Duchess*]

[*Enter Duchess, Antonio, and Cariola*]

DUCHESS. Bring me the Casket hither, and the Glasse;
You get no lodging here, to-night (my Lord.)

ANTONIO. Indeed, I must perswade one:

DUCHESS. Very good!
I hope in time 'twill grow into a custome,
That Noblemen shall come with cap, and knee,
To purchase a nights lodging, of their wives.

ANTONIO. I must lye here.

DUCHESS. Must? you are a Lord of Misse-rule.

ANTONIO. Indeed, my Rule is onely in the night.

DUCHESS. To what use will you put me?—

ANTONIO. Wee'll sleepe together:

DUCHESS. Alas, what pleasure can two Lovers find in sleepe?

CARIOLA. My Lord, I lye with her often: and I know
She'll much disquiet you:

ANTONIO. See, you are complain'd of.

CARIOLA. For she's the sprawlingst bedfellow.

ANTONIO. I shall like her the better for that.

CARIOLA. Sir, shall I aske you a question?

ANTONIO. I pray thee *Cariola.*

CARIOLA. Wherefore still when you lie with my Lady
Doe you rise so early?

ANTONIO. Labouring men
Count the Clocke oftnest *Cariola,*
Are glad when their task's ended.

DUCHESS. I'll stop your mouth.   [*kisses him*

ANTONIO. Nay, that's but one, *Venus* had two soft Doves
To draw her Chariot: I must have another: [*kisses her*
When wilt thou marry, *Cariola?*
  CARIOLA. Never (my Lord.)
  ANTONIO. O fie upon this single life: forgoe it:
We read how *Daphne*, for her peevish [f]light
Became a fruitlesse Bay-tree: *Siri[n]x* turn'd
To the pale empty Reede: *Anaxar[e]te*
Was frozen into Marble: whereas those
Which married, or prov'd kind unto their friends
Were, by a gracious influence, transhap'd
Into the Oliffe, Pomgranet, Mulbery:
Became Flowres, precious Stones, or eminent Starres.
  CARIOLA. This is a vaine Poetry: but I pray you tell me,
If there were propos'd me, Wisdome, Riches, and Beauty,
In three severall young men, which should I choose?
  ANTONIO. 'Tis a hard question: This was *Paris'* case
And he was blind in't, and there was great cause:
For how was't possible he could judge right,
Having three amorous Goddesses in view,
And they starcke naked? 'twas a Motion
Were able to be-night the apprehention
Of the seveerest Counsellor of Europe.
Now I looke on both your faces, so well form'd,
It puts me in mind of a question, I would aske.
  CARIOLA. What is't?
  ANTONIO. I doe wonder why hard-favour'd Ladies
For the most part, keepe worse-favour'd waieting women,
To attend them, and cannot endure faire-ones.
  DUCHESS. Oh, that's soone answer'd.
Did you ever in your life know an ill Painter
Desire to have his dwelling next doore to the shop
Of an excellent Picture-maker? 'twould disgrace
His face-making, and undoe him: I pre-thee
When were we so merry? my haire tangles.
  ANTONIO. 'Pray-thee (*Cariola*) let's steale forth the roome,
And let her talke to her selfe: I have divers times
Serv'd her the like—when she hath chafde extreamely:
I love to see her angry: softly *Cariola*.
                              [*exeunt [Antonio and Cariola]*
  DUCHESS. Doth not the colour of my haire 'gin to change?
When I waxe gray, I shall have all the Court
Powder their haire, with Arras, to be like me:

You have cause to love me, I entred you into my heart   [*enter*
Before you would vouchsafe to call for the keyes.   *Ferdinand*
We shall one day have my brothers take you napping: *unseen*
Me thinkes his Presence (being now in Court)
Should make you keepe your owne Bed: but you'll say
Love mixt with feare, is sweetest: I'll assure you
You shall get no more children till my brothers
Consent to be your Ghossips: have you lost your tongue?   [*she*
'Tis welcome: *turns and sees Ferdinand*
For know whether I am doomb'd to live, or die,
I can doe both like a Prince.   [*Ferdinand gives*
   FERDINAND. Die then, quickle: *her a ponyard*
Vertue, where art thou hid? what hideous thing
Is it, that doth ecclipze thee?
   DUCHESS. 'Pray sir heare me:
   FERDINAND. Or is it true, thou art but a bare name,
And no essentiall thing?
   DUCHESS. Sir!
   FERDINAND. Doe not speake.
   DUCHESS. No sir:
I will plant my soule in mine eares, to heare you.
   FERDINAND. Oh most imperfect light of humaine reason,
That mak'st [us] so unhappy, to foresee
What we can least prevent: Pursue thy wishes:
And glory in them: there's in shame no comfort,
But to be past all bounds, and sence of shame.
   DUCHESS. I pray sir, heare me: I am married—
   FERDINAND. So!
   DUCHESS. Happily, not to your liking: but for that
Alas: your sheeres doe come untimely now
To clip the birds wings, that's already flowne:
Will you see my Husband?
   FERDINAND. Yes, if I could change
Eyes with a Basilisque:
   DUCHESS. Sure, you came hither
By his con[fe]deracy.
   FERDINAND. The howling of a Wolfe
Is musicke to the[e] (schrech-Owle) pre'thee peace:
What ere thou art, that hast enjoy'd my sister,
(For I am sure thou hearst me) for thine owne sake
Let me not know thee: I came hither, prepar'd
To worke thy discovery: yet am now perswaded
It would beget such violent effects

As would damp[n]e us both: I would not for ten Millions
I had beheld thee: therefore use all meanes
I never may have knowledge of thy name;
Enjoy thy lust still, and a wret[c]hed life,
On that condition: And for thee (vilde woman,)
If thou doe wish thy Leacher may grow old
In thy Embracements, I would have thee build
Such a roome for him, as our Anchorites
To holier use enhabite: Let not the Sunne
Shine on him, till he's dead: Let Dogs, and Monkeys
Onely converse with him, and such dombe things
To whom Nature denies use to sound his name.
Doe not keepe a Paraqueto, least she learne it;
If thou doe love him, cut out thine owne tongue
Least it bewray him.
    DUCHESS. Why might not I marry?
I have not gone about, in this, to create
Any new world, or custome.
    FERDINAND. Thou art undone:
And thou hast ta'ne that massiy sheete of lead
That hid thy husbands bones, and foulded it
About my heart.
    DUCHESS. Mine bleedes for't.
    FERDINAND. Thine? thy heart?
What should I nam't, unlesse a hollow bullet
Fill'd with unquenchable wild-fire?
    DUCHESS. You are, in this
Too strict: and were you not my Princely brother
I would say to[o] wilfull: My reputation
Is safe.
    FERDINAND. Dost thou know what reputation is?
I'll tell thee—to small purpose, since th'instruction
Comes now too late:
Upon a time Reputation, Love, and Death,
Would travell ore the world: and [i]t was concluded
That they should part, and take three severall wayes:
Death told them, they should find him in great Battailes:
Or Cities plagu'd with plagues: Love gives them councell
To enquire for him 'mongst unambitious shepheards,
Where dowries were not talk'd of: and sometimes
'Mongst quiet kindred, that had nothing left
By their dead Parents: stay (quoth Reputation)
Doe not forsake me: for it is my nature

If once I part from any man I meete,
I am never found againe: And so, for you:
You have [shooke] hands with Reputation,
And made him invisible: So fare you well.
I will never see you more.
    DUCHESS. Why should onely I,
Of all the other Princes of the World
Be cas'de-up, like a holy Relique? I have youth,
And a litle beautie.
    FERDINAND. So you have some Virgins,
That are Witches: I will never see thee more.   *[exit: enter*
                           Antonio with a Pistoll, [and Cariola]
    DUCHESS. You saw this apparition?
    ANTONIO. Yes: we are
Betraid; how came he hither? I should turne   *[he points the*
This, to thee, for that.   *pistol at Cariola*
    CARIOLA. Pray sir doe: and when
That you have cleft my heart, you shall read there,
Mine innocence:
    DUCHESS. That Gallery gave him entrance.
    ANTONIO. I would this terrible thing would come againe,
That (standing on my Guard) I might relate
My warrantable love: ha, what meanes this?
    DUCHESS. He left this with me: *[she shewes the*
    ANTONIO. And it seemes, did wish   *poniard*
You would use it on your selfe?
    DUCHESS. His Action seem'd
To intend so much.
    ANTONIO. This hath a handle to't,
As well as a point—turne it towards him, and
So fasten the keene edge, in his rancke gall: *[knocking within*
How now? who knocks? more Earthquakes?
    DUCHESS. I stand
As if a Myne, beneath my feete, were ready
To be blowne up.
    CARIOLA. 'Tis *Bosola*:
    DUCHESS. Away!—
Oh misery, me thinkes unjust actions
Should weare these masques, and curtaines; and not we:
You must instantly part hence: I have fashion'd it already.
                        [exit Antonio [enter Bosola]
    BOSOLA. The Duke your brother is ta'ne up in a whirlewind—
Hath tooke horse, and's rid poast to Rome.

DUCHESS. So late?

BOSOLA. He told me, (as he mounted into th'sadle,)
You were undone.

DUCHESS. Indeed, I am very neere it.

BOSOLA. What's the matter?

DUCHESS. *Antonio*, the master of our house-hold
Hath dealt so falsely with me, in's accounts:
My brother stood engag'd with me for money
Ta'ne up of certaine Neopolitane Jewes,
And *Antonio* lets the Bonds be forfeyt.

BOSOLA. S[t]range: [*aside*] this is cunning:

DUCHESS. And hereupon
My brothers Bills at Naples are protested
Against: call up our Officers.

BOSOLA. I shall.   [*exit: enter Antonio*

DUCHESS. The place that you must flye to, is *Ancona*—
Hire a house there. I'll send after you
My Treasure, and my Jew[e]lls: our weake safetie
Runnes upon engenous wheeles: short sillables,
Must stand for periods: I must now accuse you
Of such a fained crime, as *Tasso* calls
Magnanima Mensogna: a Noble Lie,
'Cause it must shield our honors: harke they are comming.
                                    [*enter Bosola and Officers*

ANTONIO. Will your Grace heare me?

DUCHESS. I have got well by you: you have yeelded me
A million of losse; I am like to inherit
The peoples curses for your Stewardship:
You had the tricke, in Audit time to be sicke,
Till I had sign'd your *Quietus*; and that cur'de you
Without helpe of a Doctor. Gentlemen,
I would have this man be an example to you all:
So shall you hold my favour: I pray let him;
For h'as done that (alas) you would not thinke of,
And (because I intend to be rid of him)
I meane not to publish: use your fortune else-where.

ANTONIO. I am strongly arm'd to brooke my over-throw,
As commonly men beare with a hard yeere:
I will not blame the cause on't; but doe thinke
The necessitie of my malevolent starre
Procures this, not her humour: O the inconstant,
And rotten ground of service, you may see:
'Tis ev'n like him, that in a winter night

Takes a long slumber, ore a dying fire;
[As] loth to part from't: yet parts thence as cold,
As when he first sat downe.

DUCHESS. We doe confi[s]cate
(Towards the satisfying of your accounts)
All that you have.

ANTONIO. I am all yours: and 'tis very fit
All mine should be so.

DUCHESS. So, sir; you have your Passe.

ANTONIO. You may see (Gentlemen) what 'tis to serve
A Prince with body, and soule.   [exit

BOSOLA. Heere's an example, for extortion; what moysture is
drawne out of the Sea, when fowle weather comes, powres downe,
and runnes into the Sea againe.

DUCHESS. I would know what are your opinions
Of this *Antonio*.

2. OFFICER. He could not abide to see a Pigges head gaping—
I thought your Grace would finde him a Jew:

3. OFFICER. I would you had bin his Officer, for your owne sake.

4. OFFICER. You would have had more money.

1. OFFICER. He stop'd his eares with blacke wooll: and (to
those came to him for money) said he was thicke of hearing.

2. OFFICER. Some said he was an hermophrodite, for he could
not abide a woman.

4. OFFICER. How scurvy prowd he would looke, when the
Treasury was full: Well, let him goe:

1. OFFICER. Yes, and the chippings of the Buttrey fly after
him, to scowre his gold Chaine.

DUCHESS. Leave us: what doe you thinke of these?   [*exeunt*
BOSOLA. That these are Rogues; that in's prosperitie,   *Officers*
But to have waited on his fortune, could have wish'd
His durty Stirrop rivited through their noses:
And follow'd after's Mule, like a Beare in a Ring.
Would have prostituted their daughters, to his Lust:
Made their first-borne Intelligencers: thought none happy
But such as were borne under his bless'd Plannet
And wore his Livory: and doe these Lyce drop off now?
Well, never looke to have the like againe;
He hath left a sort of flattring rogues behind him,
Their doombe must follow: Princes pay flatterers,
In their owne money: Flatterers dissemble their vices,
And they dissemble their lies, that's Justice:
Alas, poore gentleman!—

DUCHESS. Poore! he hath amply fill'd his cofers.

BOSOLA. Sure he was too honest: *Pluto* the god of riches,
When he's sent (by *Jupiter*) to any man
He goes limping, to signifie that wealth
That comes on god's name, comes slowly, but when he's sent
[On] the divells arrand, he rides poast, and comes in by scuttles:
Let me shew you, what a most unvalu'd jewell,
You have (in a wanton humour) throwne away,
To blesse the man shall find him: He was an excellent
Courtier, and most faithfull, a souldier, that thought it
As beastly to know his owne value too little,
As devillish to acknowledge it too much,
Both his vertue, and forme, deserv'd a farre better fortune:
His discourse rather delighted to judge it selfe, then shew it selfe.
His breast was fill'd with all perfection,
And yet it seem'd a private whispring roome.
It made so little noyse of't.

DUCHESS. But he was basely descended.

BOSOLA. Will you make your selfe a mercinary herald,
Rather to examine mens pedegrees, then vertues?
You shall want him,
For know an honest states-man to a Prince,
Is like a Cedar, planted by a Spring,
The Spring bathes the trees roote, the gratefull tree
Rewards it with his shadow: you have not done so—
I would sooner swim to the *Bermoothes* on
Two Politisians' rotten bladders, tide
Together with an Intelligencers hart-string
Then depend on so changeable a Princes favour.
Fare-thee-well (*Antonio*) since the mallice of the world
Would needes downe with thee, it cannot be sayd yet
That any ill happened unto thee,
Considering thy fall was accompanied with vertue.

DUCHESS. Oh, you render me excellent Musicke.

BOSOLA. Say you?

DUCHESS. This good one that you speake of, is my husband.

BOSOLA. Do I not dreame? can this ambitious age
Have so much goodnes in't, as to prefer
A man, meerely for worth: without these shadowes
Of wealth and painted honors? possible?

DUCHESS. I have had three children by him.

BOSOLA. Fortunate Lady,
For you have made your private nuptiall bed

The humble, and faire Seminary of peace,
No question but: many an unbenific'd Scholler
Shall pray for you, for this deed, and rejoyce
That some preferment in the world can yet
Arise from merit. The virgins of your land
(That have no dowries) shall hope your example
Will raise them to rich husbands: Should you want
Souldiers 'twould make the very *Turkes* and *Moores*
Turne Christians, and serve you for this act.
Last, the neglected Poets of your time,
In honour of this trophee of a man,
Rais'd by that curious engine, (your white hand)
Shall thanke you, in your grave, for't; and make that
More reverend then all the Cabinets
Of living Princes: For *Antonio*—
His fame shall likewise flow from many a pen,
When Heralds shall want coates, to sell to men.
   DUCHESS. As I taste comfort, in this friendly speech,
So would I finde concealement.
   BOSOLA. O the secret of my Prince,
Which I will weare on th'in-side of my heart.
   DUCHESS. You shall take charge of all my coyne, and jewels,
And follow him, for he retires himselfe
To *Ancona*.
   BOSOLA. So.
   DUCHESS. Wh[i]ther, within few dayes,
I meane to follow thee.
   BOSOLA. Let me thinke:
I would wish your Grace, to faigne a Pilgrimage
To our Lady of *Loretto*, (scarce seaven leagues
From faire *Ancona*)—so may you depart
Your Country, with more honour, and your flight
Will seeme a Princely progresse, retaining
Your usuall traine about you.
   DUCHESS. Sir, your direction
Shall lead me, by the hand.
   CARIOLA. In my opinion,
She were better progresse to the bathes at *Leuca*,
Or go visit the *Spaw*
In *Germany*, for (if you will beleeve me)
I do not like this jesting with religion,
This faigned Pilgrimage.
   DUCHESS. Thou art a superstitious foole,

Prepare us instantly for our departure:
Past sorrowes, let us moderately lament them,
For those to come, seeke wisely, to prevent them.   [*exit Duchess,*
  BOSOLA. A Polititian is the divells quilted anvell,   *with*
He fashions all sinnes on him, and the blowes   *Cariola*
Are never heard—he may worke in a Ladies Chamber,
(As here for proofe)—what rests, but I reveale
All to my Lord? oh, this base quality
Of Intelligencer! why, every Quality i'th'world
Preferres but gaine, or commendation:
Now for this act, I am certaine to be rais'd,
"And men that paint weedes, (to the life) are prais'd.   [*exit*

SCENA III

[*Rome. The Cardinal's Palace*]

[*Enter*] Cardinall, Ferdinand, Mallateste, Pescara, Silvo, Delio

CARDINALL. Must we turne Souldier then?
  MALLATESTE. The Emperour,
Hearing your worth that way, (ere you attain'd
This reverend garment,) joynes you in commission
With the right fortunate souldier, the Marquis of *Pescara,*
And the famous *Lanoy.*
  CARDINALL. He that had the honour
Of taking the *French* King Prisoner?
  MALLATESTE. The same—
Here's a plot drawne, for a new Fortification,
At *Naples.*
  FERDINAND. This great Count *Mala[teste],* I perceive
Hath got employment?
  DELIO. No employment (my Lord)—
A marginall note in the muster-booke, that he is
A voluntary Lord.
  FERDINAND. He's no Souldier?
  DELIO. He has worne gun-powder, in's hollow tooth,
For the tooth-ache.
  SILVIO. He comes to the leaguer, with a full intent,
To eate fresh beefe, and garlicke, meanes to stay
Till the sent be gon, and straight returne to Court.

DELIO. He hath read all the late service,
As the City Chronicle relates it,
And keepe[s] two [Painters] going, onely to expresse
Battailes in modell.

SILVIO. Then he'l fight by the booke.

DELIO. By the Almanacke, I thinke,
To choose good dayes, and shun the Criticall.
That's his mistris' skarfe.

SILVIO. Yes, he protests
He would do much for that taffita—

DELIO. I thinke he would run away from a battaile
To save it from taking prisoner.

SILVIO. He is horribly afraid,
Gun-powder will spoile the perfume on't—

DELIO. I saw a Duch-man breake his pate once
For calling him pot-gun—he made his head
Have a boare in't, like a musket.

SILVIO. I would he had made a touch-hole to't.
He is indeede a guarded sumpter-cloath
Onely for the remoove of the Court.   [enter Bosola

PESCARA. Bosola arriv'd? what should be the businesse?
Some falling out amongst the Cardinalls.
These factions amongst great men, they are like
Foxes—when their heads are devided
They carry fire in their tailes, and all the Country
About them, goes to wracke for't.

SILVIO. What's that Bosola?

DELIO. I knew him in Padua, a fantasticall scholler,
Like such, who studdy to know how many knots
Was in Hercules club, of what colour Achilles beard was,
Or whether Hector were not troubled with the tooth-ach—
He hath studdied himselfe halfe bleare-ei'd, to know
The true semitry of Cæsars nose by a shooing-horne,
And this he did
To gaine the name of a speculative man.

PESCARA. Marke Prince Ferdinand,
A very Salamander lives in's eye,
To mocke the eager violence of fire.

SILVIO. That Cardinall hath made more bad faces with his
       oppression
Then ever Michael Angelo made good ones,
He lifts up's nose, like a fowle Por-pisse before
A storme—

PESCARA. The Lord *Ferdinand* laughes.

DELIO. Like a deadly Cannon,
That lightens ere it smoakes.

PESCARA. These are your true pangues of death,
The pangues of life, that strugle with great states-men—

DELIO. In such a deformed silence, witches whisper
Their charmes.

CARDINALL. Doth she make religion her riding hood
To keepe her from the sun, and tempest?

FERDINAND. That: that damnes her: Me thinkes her fault, and
        beauty
Blended together, shew like leaprosie—
The whiter, the fowler: I make it a question
Whether her beggerly brats were ever christned.

CARDINALL. I will instantly sollicite the state of *Ancona*
To have them banish'd.

FERDINAND. You are for *Loretto*?
I shall not be at your Ceremony: fare you well,
Write to the Duke of *Malfy*, my yong Nephew,
She had by her first husband, and acquaint him,
With's mothers honesty.

BOSOLA. I will.

FERDINAND. *Antonio!*
A slave, that onely smell'd of yncke, and coumpters,
And nev'r in's li[f]e, look'd like a Gentleman,
But in the audit time—go, go presently,
Draw me out an hundreth and fifty of our horse,
And meete me at the fort-bridge.   [*exeunt*

SCENA IIII

[*Loretto*]

[*Enter*] *Two Pilgrims to the Shrine of our Lady
of* Loretto

1. PILGRIM. I have not seene a goodlier Shrine then this,
Yet I have visited many.

2. PILGRIM. The Cardinall of *Arragon*
Is, this day, to resigne his Cardinals hat,
His sister Duchesse likewise is arriv'd
To pay her vow of Pilgrimage—I expect
A noble Ceremony.

1. PILGRIM. No question:———They come.

Here the Ceremony of the Cardinalls enstalment, in the habit [of] a
Souldier: perform'd in delivering up his Crosse, Hat, Robes, and
Ring, at the Shrine; and investing him with Sword, Helmet,
Sheild, and Spurs: Then Antonio, *the* Duchesse, *and their*
Children, (having presented themselves at the Shrine) are (by a
forme of Banishment in dumbe-shew, expressed towards them by
the Cardinall, and the State of Ancona) *banished: During all*
which Ceremony, this Ditty is sung (to very sollemne Musique) by
divers Church-men; and then Exeunt.

Armes, and Honors, decke thy story,
To thy Fames eternall glory,
Adverse Fortune ever flie-thee,   The Au-
No disastrous fate come nigh-thee.   thor dis-
                                               claimes
I alone will sing thy praises,   this Ditty
Whom to honour vertue raises;   to be his.
And thy study, that divine-is,
Bent to Marshiall discipline-is:
Lay aside all those robes lie by thee,
Crown thy arts, with armes: they'll beutifie thee.

O worthy of worthiest name, adorn'd in this manner,
Lead bravely thy forces on, under wars warlike banner:
O mayst thou prove fortunate, in all Marshiall courses,
Guide thou still, by skill, in artes, and forces:
Victory attend thee nigh, whilst fame sings loud thy powres,
Triumphant conquest crowne thy head, and blessings powre
              downe showres.

1. PILGRIM. Here's a strange turne of state—who would have
      thought
So great a Lady, would have match'd her selfe
Unto so meane a person? yet the Cardinall
Beares himselfe much too cruell.
      2. PILGRIM. They are banish'd.
      1. PILGRIM. But I would aske what power hath this state
Of *Ancona*, to determine of a free Prince?
      2. PILGRIM. They are a free state sir, and her brother shew'd
How that the Pope fore-hearing of her loosenesse,
Hath seaz'd into th'protection of the Church
The Dukedome, which she held as dowager.
      1. PILGRIM. But by what justice?

2. PILGRIM. Sure I thinke by none,
Only her brothers instigation.

   1. PILGRIM. What was it, with such violence he tooke
Of[f] from her finger?

   2. PILGRIM. 'Twas her wedding ring,
Which he vow'd shortly he would sacrifice
To his revenge.

   1. PILGRIM. Alasse *Antonio*,
If that a man be thrust into a well,
No matter who sets hand to't, his owne weight
Will bring him sooner to th'bottome: Come, let's hence.
Fortune makes this conclusion generall,
"All things do helpe th'unhappy man to fall.   [*exeunt*

SCENA V

[*Near Loretto*]

[*Enter*] *Antonio, Duchesse, Children,*
Cariola, Servants

DUCHESS. Banish'd *Ancona*!

   ANTONIO. Yes, you see what powre
Lightens in great mens breath.

   DUCHESS. Is all our traine
Shrunke to this poore remainder?

   ANTONIO. These poore men,
(Which have got little in your service) vow
To take your fortune: But your wiser buntings
Now they are fledg'd, are gon.

   DUCHESS. They have done wisely—
This puts me in minde of death, Physitians thus,
With their hands full of money, use to give ore
Their Patients.

   ANTONIO. Right the fashion of the world—
From decaide fortunes, every flatterer shrinkes,
Men cease to build, where the foundation sinkes.

   DUCHESS. I had a very strange dreame to-night.

   ANTONIO. What was't?

   DUCHESS. Me thought I wore my Coronet of State,
And on a sudaine all the Diamonds
Were chang'd to Pearles.

ANTONIO. My Interpretation
Is you'll weepe shortly, for to me, the pearles
Doe signifie your teares:
DUCHESS. The Birds, that live i'th field
On the wilde benefit of Nature, live
Happier then we; for they may choose their Mates,
And carroll their sweet pleasures to the Spring: [enter Bosola
BOSOLA. You are happily ore-ta'ne.   *with a letter*
DUCHESS. From my brother?
BOSOLA. Yes, from the Lord *Ferdinand*...your brother,
All love, and safetie—
DUCHESS. Thou do'st blanch mischiefe—
Wouldst make it white: See, see; like to calme weather
At Sea, before a tempest, false hearts speake faire
To those they intend most mischiefe.
          [*Reads*] A Letter.
Send Antonio *to me*; *I want his head in a busines*:
A politicke equivocation—
He doth not want your councell, but your head;
That is, he cannot sleepe till you be dead.
And here's annother Pitfall, that's strew'd ore
With Roses: marke it, 'tis a cunning one.
I stand ingaged for your husband, for severall debts at Naples: *let not
that trouble him, I had rather have his heart, then his mony.*
And I beleeve so too.
BOSOLA. What doe you beleeve?
DUCHESS. That he so much distrusts my husbands love,
He will by no meanes beleeve his heart is with him
Untill he see it: The Divell is not cunning enough
To circumvent us in Ridles.
BOSOLA. Will you reject that noble, and free league
Of amitie, and love which I present you?
DUCHESS. Their league is like that of some politick Kings
Onely to make themselves of strength, and powre
To be our after-ruine: tell them so;
BOSOLA. And what from you?
ANTONIO. Thus tell him: I will not come.
BOSOLA. And what of this?
ANTONIO. My brothers have dispers'd
Blood-hounds abroad; which till I heare are muzell'd,
No truce, though hatch'd with nere such politick skill
Is safe, that hangs upon our enemies will.
I'll not come at them.

FDM   4

BOSOLA. This proclaimes your breeding.
Every small thing drawes a base mind to feare:
As the Adamant drawes yron: fare you well sir,
You shall shortly heare from's.   [*exit*

DUCHESS. I suspect some Ambush:
Therefore by all my love...I doe conjure you
To take your eldest sonne, and flye towards *Millaine*;
Let us not venture all this poore remainder
In one unlucky bottom.

ANTONIO. You councell safely:
Best of my life, farewell: Since we must part,
Heaven hath a hand in't: but no otherwise,
Then as some curious Artist takes in sunder
A Clocke, or Watch, when it is out of frame
To bring't in better order.

DUCHESS. I know not which is best,
To see you dead, or part with you: Farewell Boy.
Thou art happy, that thou hast not understanding
To know thy misery: For all our wit
And reading, brings us to a truer sence
Of sorrow: In the eternall Church, Sir,
I doe hope we shall not part thus.

ANTONIO. Oh, be of comfort,
Make Patience a noble fortitude:
And thinke not how unkindly we are us'de:
"Man (like to *Cassia*) is prov'd best, being bruiz'd.

DUCHESS. Must I like to a slave-borne Russian,
Account it praise to suffer tyranny?
And yet (O Heaven) thy heavy hand is in't.
I have seene my litle boy oft scourge his top,
And compar'd my selfe to't: naught made me ere
Go right, but Heavens scourge-sticke.

ANTONIO. Doe not weepe:
Heaven fashion'd us of nothing: and we strive,
To bring our selves to nothing: farewell *Cariola*,
And thy sweet armefull: if I doe never see thee more,
Be a good Mother to your litle ones,
And save them from the Tiger: fare you well.

DUCHESS. Let me looke upon you once more: for that
        speech
Came from a dying father: your kisse is colder
Then that I have seene an holy Anchorite
Give to a dead mans skull.

ANTONIO.   My heart is turnde to a heavy lumpe of lead,
With which I sound my danger: fare you well.   [*exit,* [*with son*]
    DUCHESS.   My Laurell is all withered.
    CARIOLA.   Looke (Madam) what a troope of armed men
Make toward us.   [*enter Bosola with a Guard,* [*with Vizards*]
    DUCHESS.   O, they are very welcome:
When Fortunes wheele is over-charg'd with Princes,
The waight makes it move swift. I wo[u]ld have my ruine
Be sudden: I am your adventure, am I not?
    BOSOLA.   You are, you must see your husband no more—
    DUCHESS.   What Divell art thou, that counterfeits heavens
        thunder?
    BOSOLA.   Is that terrible? I would have you tell me whether
Is that note worse, that frights the silly birds
Out of the corne; or that which doth allure them
To the nets? you have hearkned to the last too much.
    DUCHESS.   O misery: like to a rusty ore-char[g]'d Cannon,
Shall I never flye in peeces? come: to what Prison?
    BOSOLA.   To none:
    DUCHESS.   Wh[i]ther then?
    BOSOLA.   To your Pallace.
    DUCHESS.   I have heard that *Charons* boate serves to convay
All ore the dismall Lake, but brings none backe againe.
    BOSOLA.   Your brothers meane you safety, and pitie.
    DUCHESS.   Pitie!
With such a pitie men preserve alive
Pheasants, and Quailes, when they are not fat enough
To be eaten.
    BOSOLA.   These are your children?
    DUCHESS.   Yes:
    BOSOLA.   Can they pratle?
    DUCHESS.   No:
But I intend, since they were borne accurs'd;
Cursses shall be their first language.
    BOSOLA.   Fye (Madam)
Forget this base, low-fellow.
    DUCHESS.   Were I a man:
I'll'd beat that counterfeit face, into thy other—
    BOSOLA.   One of no Birth.
    DUCHESS.   Say that he was borne meane...
Man is most happy, when's owne actions
Be arguments, and examples of his Vertue.
    BOSOLA.   A barren, beggerly vertue.

DUCHESS. I pre-thee who is greatest, can you tell?
Sad tales befit my woe: I'll tell you one.
A Salmon, as she swam unto the Sea,
Met with a Dog-fish; who encounters her
With this rough language: why art thou so bold
To mixe thy selfe with our high state of floods
Being no eminent Courtier, but one
That for the calmest, and fresh time o'th' yeere
Do'st live in shallow Rivers, rank'st thy selfe
With silly Smylts, and Shrympes? and darest thou
Passe by our Dog-ship, without reverence?
O (Quoth the Salmon) sister, be at peace:
Thanke *Jupiter*, we both have pass'd the Net—
Our value never can be truely knowne,
Till in the Fishers basket we be showne,
I'th' Market then my price may be the higher,
Even when I am neerest to the Cooke, and fire.
So, to Great men, the Morrall may be stretched.
"Men oft are valued high, when th'are most wretch[e]d.
But come: wh[i]ther you please: I am arm'd 'gainst misery:
Bent to all swaies of the Oppressors will.
There's no deepe Valley, but neere some great Hill.   [*exit*

ACTUS IIII. SCENA I

[*Amalfi. The Palace of the Duchess*]

[*Enter Ferdinand and Bosola*]

FERDINAND. How doth our sister Dutchesse beare her selfe
In her imprisonment?
   BOSOLA. Nobly: I'll describe her:
She's sad, as one long us'd to't: and she seemes
Rather to welcome the end of misery
Then shun it: a behaviour so noble,
As gives a majestie to adversitie:
You may discerne the shape of lovelinesse
More perfect, in her teares, then in her smiles;
She will muse foure houres together: and her silence,
(Me thinkes) expresseth more, then if she spake.
   FERDINAND. Her mellancholly seemes to be fortifide
With a strange disdaine.
   BOSOLA. 'Tis so: and this restraint
(Like English Mastiffes, that grow feirce with tying)
Makes her too passionately apprehend
Those pleasures she's kept from.
   FERDINAND. Curse upon her!
I will no longer study in the booke
Of anothers heart: informe her what I told you.   [*exit: enter*
   BOSOLA. All comfort to your Grace;   *Duchess and Attendants*
   DUCHESS. I will have none:
'Pray-thee, why do'st thou wrap thy poysond Pilles
In Gold, and Sugar?
   BOSOLA. Your elder brother the Lord *Ferdinand*
Is come to visite you: and sends you word,
'Cause once he rashly made a solemne vowe
Never to see you more; he comes i'th' night:

And prayes you (gently) neither Torch, nor Taper
Shine in your Chamber: he will kisse your hand:
And reconcile himselfe: but, for his vowe,
He dares not see you:
   DUCHESS. At his pleasure:
Take hence the lights: he's come.   [*exeunt Servants with lights;*
   FERDINAND. Where are you?   *enter Ferdinand*
   DUCHESS. Here sir:
   FERDINAND. This darkenes suites you well.
   DUCHESS. I would aske you pardon:
   FERDINAND. You have it;
For I account it the honorabl'st revenge
Where I may kill, to pardon: where are your Cubbs?
   DUCHESS. Whom!   FERDINAND. Call them your children;
For though our nationall law distinguish Bastards
From true legitimate issue: compassionate nature
Makes them all equall.
   DUCHESS. Doe you visit me for this?
You violate a Sacrament o'th' Church
Shall make you howle in hell for't.
   FERDINAND. It had bin well,
Could you have liv'd thus alwayes: for indeed
You were too much i'th' light: But no more—
I come to seale my peace with you: here's a hand,   [*gives her*
To which you have vow'd much love: the Ring upon't *a dead*
You gave.   *mans*
   DUCHESS. I affectionately kisse it: *hand*
   FERDINAND. 'Pray doe: and bury the print of it in your
        heart:
I will leave this Ring with you, for a Love-token:
And the hand, as sure as the ring: and doe not doubt
But you shall have the heart too: when you need a friend,
Send it to him; that ow'de it: you shall see
Whether he can ayd you.
   DUCHESS. You are very cold.
I feare you are not well after your travell:
Hah? lights: oh horrible!
   FERDINAND. / Let her have lights enough.   [*exit:* [*re-enter*
                                   Servants with lights
   DUCHESS. What witch-craft doth he practise, that he hath left
A dead-mans hand here?————*Here is discover'd, (behind a
Travers;) the artificiall figures of* Antonio, *and his children;
appearing as if they were dead.*

BOSOLA. Looke you: here's the peece, from which 'twas ta'ne;
He doth present you this sad spectacle,
That now you know directly they are dead,
Hereafter you may (wisely) cease to grieve
For that which cannot be recovered.

DUCHESS. There is not betweene heaven, and earth one wish
I stay for after this: it wastes me more,
Then were't my picture, fashion'd out of wax,
Stucke with a magicall needle, and then buried
In some fowle dung-hill: and yond's an excellent property
For a tyrant, which I would account mercy—

BOSOLA. What's that?

DUCHESS. If they would bind me to that liveles truncke,
And let me freeze to death.

BOSOLA. Come, you must live.

DUCHESS. That's the greatest torture soules feele in hell,
In hell: that they must live, and cannot die:
Portia, I'll new kindle thy Coales againe,
And revive the rare, and almost dead example
Of a loving wife.

BOSOLA. O fye: despaire? remember
You are a Christian.

DUCHESS. The Church enjoynes fasting:
I'll starve my selfe to death.

BOSOLA. Leave this vaine sorrow;
Things being at the worst, begin to mend: the Bee
When he hath shot his sting into your hand
May then play with your eye-lyd.

DUCHESS. Good comfortable fellow
Perswade a wretch that's broke upon the wheele
To have all his bones new set: entreate him live,
To be executed againe: who must dispatch me?
I account this world a tedious Theatre,
For I doe play a part in't 'gainst my will.

BOSOLA. Come, be of comfort, I will save your life.

DUCHESS. Indeed I have not leysure to tend so small a busines.

BOSOLA. Now, by my life, I pitty you.

DUCHESS. Thou art a foole then,
To wast thy pitty on a thing so wretch'd
As cannot pitty it[self]: I am full of daggers:
Puffe: let me blow these vipers from me.
What are you?   [*she turns suddenly to a Servant*
SERVANT. One that wishes you long life.

DUCHESS. I would thou wert hang'd for the horrible curse
Thou hast given me: I shall shortly grow one
Of the miracles of pitty: I'll goe pray: No,
I'll goe curse:

BOSOLA. Oh fye!

DUCHESS. I could curse the Starres.

BOSOLA. Oh fearefull!

DUCHESS. And those three smyling seasons of the yeere
Into a Russian winter: nay the world
To its first Chaos.

BOSOLA. Looke you, the Starres shine still:

DUCHESS. Oh, but you must remember, my curse hath a great
            way to goe:
Plagues, (that make lanes through largest families)
Consume them!

BOSOLA. Fye Lady!

DUCHESS. Let them like tyrants
Never be remembred, but for the ill they have done:
Let all the zealous prayers of mortefied
Church-men forget them—

BOSOLA. O uncharitable!

DUCHESS. Let heaven, a little while, cease crowning Martirs
To punish them:
Goe, howle them this: and say I long to bleed—
"It is some mercy, when men kill with speed.

                    [exit, [with Servants; re-enter Ferdinand

FERDINAND. Excellent; as I would wish: she's plagu'd in Art.
These presentations are but fram'd in wax,
By the curious Master in that Qualitie,
Vincentio Lauriola, and she takes them
For true substantiall Bodies.

BOSOLA. Why doe you doe this?

FERDINAND. To bring her to despaire.

BOSOLA. 'Faith, end here:
And go no farther in your cruelty—
Send her a penetentiall garment, to put on,
Next to her delicate skinne, and furnish her
With beades, and prayer bookes.

FERDINAND. Damne her, that body of hers,
While that my blood ran pure in't, was more worth
Then that which thou wouldst comfort, (call'd a soule)—
I will send her masques of common Curtizans,
Have her meate serv'd up by baudes, and ruffians,

And ('cause she'll needes be mad) I am resolv'd
To remove forth the common Hospitall
All the mad-folke, and place them neere her lodging:
There let them practise together, sing, and daunce,
And act their gambols to the full o'th'moone:
If she can sleepe the better for it, let her,
Your worke is almost ended.

    BOSOLA. Must I see her againe?

    FERDINAND. Yes.   BOSOLA. Never.

    FERDINAND. You must.

    BOSOLA. Never in mine owne shape,
That's forfeited, by my intelligence,
And this last cruell lie: when you send me next,
The businesse shalbe comfort.

    FERDINAND. Very likely!—
Thy pity is nothing of kin to thee: *Antonio*
Lurkes about *Millaine*, thou shalt shortly thither,
To feede a fire, as great as my revenge,
Which nev'r will slacke, till it have spent his fuell—
"Intemperate agues, make Physitians cruell.   *[exeunt*

SCENA II

[The Same]

[Enter Duchess and Cariola]

    DUCHESS. What hideous noyse was that?

    CARIOLA. 'Tis the wild consort
Of Mad-men (Lady) which your Tyrant brother
Hath plac'd about your lodging: This tyranny,
I thinke was never practis'd till this howre.

    DUCHESS. Indeed I thanke him: nothing but noyce, and folly
Can keepe me in my right wits, whereas reason
And silence, make me starke mad: Sit downe,
Discourse to me some dismall Tragedy.

    CARIOLA. O 'twill encrease your mellancholly.

    DUCHESS. Thou art deceiv'd,
To heare of greater griefe, would lessen mine—
This is a prison?   CARIOLA. Yes, but you shall live
To shake this durance off.   DUCHESS. Thou art a foole,
The Robin red-brest, and the Nightingale,
Never live long in cages.   CARIOLA. Pray drie your eyes.

What thinke you of, Madam?   DUCHESS. Of nothing:
When I muse thus, I sleepe.
    CARIOLA. Like a mad-man, with your eyes open?
    DUCHESS. Do'st thou thinke we shall know one another,
In th'other world?   CARIOLA. Yes, out of question.
    DUCHESS. O that it were possible we might
But hold some two dayes conference with the dead,
From them, I should learne somewhat, I am sure
I never shall know here: I'll tell thee a miracle—
I am not mad yet, to my cause of sorrow.
Th'heaven ore my head, seemes made of molt[e]n brasse,
The earth of flaming sulphure, yet I am not mad:
I am acquainted with sad misery,
As the tan'd galley-slave is with his Oare,
Necessity makes me suffer constantly,
And custome makes it easie—who do I looke like now?
    CARIOLA. Like to your picture in the gallery,
A deale of life in shew, but none in practise:
Or rather like some reverend monument
Whose ruines are even pittied.   DUCHESS. Very proper:
And Fortune seemes onely to have her eie-sight,
To behold my Tragedy:
How now, what noyce is that?   [enter Servant
    SERVANT. I am come to tell you,
Your brother hath entended you some sport:
A great Physitian, when the Pope was sicke
Of a deepe mellancholly, presented him
With severall sorts of mad-men, which wilde object
(Being full of change, and sport,) forc'd him to laugh,
And so th'impost-hume broke: the selfe same cure,
The Duke intends on you.
    DUCHESS. Let them come in.
    SERVANT. There's a mad Lawyer, and a secular Priest,
A Doctor that hath forfeited his wits
By jealousie: an Astrologian,
That in his workes, sayd such a day o'th'moneth
Should be the day of doome; and fayling of't,
Ran mad: an English Taylor, crais'd i'th'braine,
With the studdy of new fashion: a gentleman usher
Quite beside himselfe, with care to keepe in minde,
The number of his Ladies salutations,
Or "how do you", she employ'd him in each morning:
A Farmer too, (an excellent knave in graine)

Mad, 'cause he was hindred transportation,
And let one Broaker (that's mad) loose to these,
You'ld thinke the divell were among them.
    DUCHESS. Sit *Cariola*: let them loose when you please,
For I am chain'd to endure all your tyranny.   *[enter Madmen*

> *Here (by a Mad-man) this song is sung, to a dismall*
> *kind of Musique.*
>
> *O let us howle, some heavy note,*
>   *some deadly-dogged howle,*
> *Sounding, as from the threatning throat,*
>   *of beastes, and fatall fowle.*
> *As Ravens, Schrich-owles, Bulls, and Beares,*
>   *We'll b[e]ll, and bawle our parts,*
> *Till yerk-some noyce have cloy'd your eares,*
>   *and corasiv'd your hearts.*
> *At last when as our quire wants breath,*
>   *our bodies being blest,*
> *We'll sing like Swans, to welcome death,*
>   *and die in love and rest.*

    1. MAD-MAN. [*Astrologer.*] Doomes-day not come yet? I'll draw it neerer by a perspective, or make a glasse, that shall set all the world on fire upon an instant: I cannot sleepe, my pillow is stuff't with a littour of Porcupines.

    2. MAD-MAN. [*Lawyer.*] Hell is a meere glasse-house, where the divells are continually blowing up womens soules, on hollow yrons, and the fire never goes out.

    3. MAD-MAN. [*Priest.*] I will lie with every woman in my parish the tenth night: I will tithe them over, like hay-cockes.

    4. MAD-MAN. [*Doctor.*] Shall my Pothecary out-go me, because I am a Cuck-old? I have found out his roguery: he makes allom of his wives urin, and sells it to Puritaines, that have sore throates with over-strayning.

    1. MAD-MAN. I have skill in Harroldry.

    2. Hast?

    1. You do give for your creast a wood-cockes head, with the Braines pickt out on't, you are a very ancient Gentleman.

    3. Greeke is turn'd Turke, we are onely to be sav'd by the Helvetian translation.

    1. Come on Sir, I will lay the law to you.

    2. Oh, rather lay a corazive—the law will eate to the bone.

    3. He that drinkes but to satisfie nature is damn'd.

4. If I had my glasse here, I would shew a sight should make all the women here call me mad Doctor.

1. What's he, a rope-maker?   [*pointing at the Priest*

2. No, no, no, a snufling knave, that while he shewes the tombes, will have his hand in a wenches placket.

3. Woe to the Caroach, that brought home my wife from the Masque, at three a clocke in the morning, it had a large Feather-bed in it.

4. I have paired the divells nayles forty times, roasted them in Ravens egges, and cur'd agues with them.

3. Get me three hundred milch bats, to make possets, to procure sleepe.

4. All the Colledge may throw their caps at me, I have made a Soape-boyler costive, it was my master-peece:——*Here the Daunce consisting of 8. Mad-men, with musicke answerable thereunto, after which,* Bosola (*like an old man*) *enters.*

DUCHESS. Is he mad to[o]?

SERVANT. 'Pray question him: I'll leave you.   [*exeunt Servant*

BOSOLA. I am come to make thy tombe.   *and Madmen*

DUCHESS. Hah, my tombe?
Thou speak'st, as if I lay upon my death bed,
Gasping for breath: do'st thou perceive me sicke?

BOSOLA. Yes, and the more dangerously, since thy sicknesse is insensible.

DUCHESS. Thou art not mad sure, do'st know me?

BOSOLA. Yes.   DUCHESS. Who am I?

BOSOLA. Thou art a box of worme-seede, at best, but a salvatory of greene mummey: what's this flesh? a little cruded milke, phantasticall puffe-paste: our bodies are weaker then those paper prisons boyes use to keepe flies in: more contemptible: since ours is to preserve earth-wormes: didst thou ever see a Larke in a cage? such is the soule in the body: this world is like her little turfe of grasse, and the Heaven ore our heades, like her looking glasse, onely gives us a miserable knowledge of the small compasse of our prison.

DUCHESS. Am not I, thy Duchesse?

BOSOLA. Thou art some great woman sure, for riot begins to sit on thy fore-head (clad in gray haires) twenty yeares sooner, then on a merry milkemaydes. Thou sleep'st worse, then if a mouse should be forc'd to take up her lodging in a cats eare: a little infant, that breedes it's teeth, should it lie with thee, would crie out, as if thou wert the more unquiet bed-fellow.

DUCHESS. I am Duchesse of *Malfy* still.

BOSOLA. That makes thy sleepes so broken:
"Glories (like glowe-wormes) afarre off, shine bright,
But look'd to neere, have neither heate, nor light.
DUCHESS. Thou art very plaine.
BOSOLA. My trade is to flatter the dead, not the living—
I am a tombe-maker.
DUCHESS. And thou com'st to make my tombe?
BOSOLA. Yes.
DUCHESS. Let me be a little merry—
Of what stuffe wilt thou make it?
BOSOLA. Nay, resolve me first, of what fashion?
DUCHESS. Why, do we grow phantasticall in our death-bed?
Do we affect fashion in the grave?
BOSOLA. Most ambitiously: Princes images on their tombes
Do not lie, as they were wont, seeming to pray
Up to heaven: but with their hands under their cheekes,
(As if they died of the tooth-ache)—they are not carved
With their eies fix'd upon the starres; but as
Their mindes were wholy bent upon the world,
The selfe-same way they seeme to turne their faces.
DUCHESS. Let me know fully therefore the effect
Of this thy dismall preparation,
This talke, fit for a charnell?
BOSOLA. Now, I shall—   *[enter Executioners with]*
Here is a present from your Princely brothers,   *a Coffin,*
And may it arrive wel-come, for it brings   *Cords, and*
Last benefit, last sorrow.   *a Bell*
DUCHESS. Let me see it—
I have so much obedience, in my blood,
I wish it in ther veines, to do them good.
BOSOLA. This is your last presence Chamber.
CARIOLA. O my sweete Lady.
DUCHESS. Peace, it affrights not me.
BOSOLA. I am the common Bell-man,   *[takes up the Bell*
That usually is sent to condemn'd persons
The night before they suffer:
DUCHESS. Even now thou said'st,
Thou wast a tombe-maker?
BOSOLA. 'Twas to bring you
By degrees to mortification: Listen.   *[rings his bell*
Hearke, now every thing is still—
The Schritch-Owle, and the whistler shrill,
Call upon our Dame, aloud,

And bid her quickly don her shrowd:
Much you had of Land and rent,
Your length in clay's now competent.
A long war disturb'd your minde,
Here your perfect peace is sign'd—
Of what is't fooles make such vaine keeping?
Sin their conception, their birth, weeping:
Their life, a generall mist of error,
Their death, a hideous storme of terror—
Strew your haire, with powders sweete:
Don cleane linnen, bath your feete,
And (the foule feend more to checke)
A crucifixe let blesse your necke,
'Tis now full tide, 'tweene night, and day,
End your groane, and come away.

    CARIOLA. Hence villaines, tyrants, murderers: alas!
What will you do with my Lady? call for helpe.

    DUCHESS. To whom, to our next neighbours? they are mad-
    folkes.

    BOSOLA. Remoove that noyse.

    DUCHESS. Farwell *Cariola*,
In my last will, I have not much to give—
A many hungry guests have fed upon me,
Thine will be a poore reversion.

    CARIOLA. I will die with her.

    DUCHESS. I pray-thee looke thou giv'st my little boy
Some sirrop, for his cold, and let the girle
Say her prayers, ere she sleepe. Now what you please,   [*Cariola*
What death?   *is forced off*

    BOSOLA. Strangling, here are your Executioners.

    DUCHESS. I forgive them:
The apoplexie, cathar, or cough o'th'loongs,
Would do as much as they do.

    BOSOLA. Doth not death fright you?

    DUCHESS. Who would be afraid on't?
Knowing to meete such excellent company
In th'other world.

    BOSOLA. Yet, me thinkes,
The manner of your death should much afflict you,
This cord should terrifie you?   DUCHESS. Not a whit—
What would it pleasure me, to have my throate cut
With diamonds? or to be smothered
With Cassia? or to be shot to death, with pearles?

I know death hath ten thousand severall doores
For men, to take their *Exits*: and 'tis found
They go on such strange geometricall hinges,
You may open them both wayes: any way, (for heaven sake)
So I were out of your whispering: Tell my brothers,
That I perceive death, (now I am well awake)
Best guift is, they can give, or I can take—
I would faine put off my last womans-fault,
I'ld not be tedious to you.
  EXECUTIONER. We are ready.
  DUCHESS. Dispose my breath, how please you, but my body
Bestow upon my women, will you? EXECUTIONER. Yes.
  DUCHESS. Pull, and pull strongly, for your able strength,
Must pull downe heaven upon me:
Yet stay, heaven gates are not so highly arch'd
As Princes pallaces—they that enter there
Must go upon their knees: Come violent death, [*she kneels*
Serve for *Mandragora*, to make me sleepe;
Go tell my brothers, when I am laid out,   [*they*
They then may feede in quiet.   *strangle her*
  BOSOLA. Where's the waiting woman?
Fetch her: Some other strangle the children: [*re-enter Execu-*
Looke you, there sleepes your mistris. *tioner with Cariola*
  CARIOLA. Oh you are damn'd
Perpetually for this: My turne is next,
Is't not so ordered? BOSOLA. Yes, and I am glad
You are so well prepar'd for't.
  CARIOLA. You are deceiv'd Sir,
I am not prepar'd for't, I will not die,
I will first come to my answere; and know
How I have offended. BOSOLA. Come, dispatch her:
You kept her counsell, now you shall keepe ours.
  CARIOLA. I will not die, I must not, I am contracted
To a young Gentle-man.
  EXECUTIONER. Here's your wedding Ring.
  CARIOLA. Let me but speake with the Duke: I'll discover
Treason to his person.
  BOSOLA. Delayes: throttle-her.
  EXECUTIONER. She bites: and scratches:
  CARIOLA. If you kill me now
I am damn'd: I have not bin at Confession
This two yeeres: BOSOLA. When!
  CARIOLA. I am quicke with child.

BOSOLA. Why then,
Your credit's sav'd: beare her into th' next roome:
                    [*they strangle her, and bear her away: enter Ferdinand*
Let this lie still.   FERDINAND. Is she dead?
    BOSOLA. Shee is what
You'll'd have her: But here begin your pitty—   [*shewes the*
Alas, how have these offended?   *children strangled*
    FERDINAND. The death
Of young Wolffes, is never to be pittied.
    BOSOLA. Fix your eye here: FERDINAND. Constantly.
    BOSOLA. Doe you not weepe?
Other sinnes onely speake; Murther shreikes out:
The Element of water moistens the Earth,
But blood flies upwards, and bedewes the Heavens.
    FERDINAND. Cover her face: Mine eyes dazell: she di'd
          yong.
    BOSOLA. I thinke not so: her infelicitie
Seem'd to have yeeres too many.
    FERDINAND. She, and I were Twinnes:
And should I die this instant, I had liv'd
Her Time to a Mynute.
    BOSOLA. It seemes she was borne first:
You have bloodely approv'd the auncient truth,
That kindred commonly doe worse ag[r]ee
Then remote strangers.
    FERDINAND. Let me see her face againe;
Why didst not thou pitty her? what an excellent
Honest man might'st thou have bin
If thou hadst borne her to some Sanctuary!
Or (bold in a good çause) oppos'd thy selfe
With thy advanced sword above thy head,
Betweene her Innocence, and my Revenge!
I bad thee, when I was distracted of my wits,
Goe kill my dearest friend, and thou hast don't.
For let me but examine well the cause;
What was the meanenes of her match to me?
Onely I must confesse, I had a hope
(Had she continu'd widow) to have gain'd
An infinite masse of Treasure by her death:
And that was the mayne cause; her Marriage—
That drew a streame of gall quite through my heart;
For thee, (as we observe in Tragedies
That a good Actor many times is curss'd

For playing a villaines part) I hate thee for't:
And (for my sake) say thou hast done much ill, well:
   BOSOLA. Let me quicken your memory: for I perceive
You are falling into ingratitude: I challenge
The reward due to my service.
   FERDINAND. I'll tell thee,
What I'll give thee—   BOSOLA. Doe:
   FERDINAND. I'll give thee a pardon
For this murther:
   BOSOLA. Hah?   FERDINAND. Yes: and 'tis
The largest bounty I can studie to doe thee.
By what authority did'st thou execute
This bloody sentence?   BOSOLA. By yours—
   FERDINAND. Mine? was I her Judge?
Did any ceremoniall forme of Law,
Doombe her to not-Being? did a compleat Jury
Deliver her conviction up i'th Court?
Where shalt thou find this [j]udgement registerd
Unlesse in hell? See: like a bloody foole
Th'hast forfeyted thy life, and thou shalt die for't.
   BOSOLA. The Office of Justice is perverted quite
When one Thiefe hangs another: who shall dare
To reveale this?   FERDINAND. Oh, I'll tell thee:
The Wolfe shall finde her Grave, and scrape it up:
Not to devoure the corpes, but to discover
The horrid murther.
   BOSOLA. You; not I, shall quake for't.
   FERDINAND. Leave me:
   BOSOLA. I will first receive my Pention.
   FERDINAND. You are a villaine:
   BOSOLA. When your Ingratitude
Is Judge, I am so.   FERDINAND. O horror!
That not the feare of him, which bindes the divels
Can prescribe man obedience.
Never looke upon me more.   BOSOLA. Why fare thee well:
Your brother, and your selfe, are worthy men;
You have a paire of hearts, are hollow Graves,
Rotten, and rotting others: and your vengeance,
(Like two chain'd bullets) still goes arme in arme—
You may be Brothers: for treason, like the plague,
Doth take much in a blood: I stand like one
That long hath ta'ne a sweet, and golden dreame.
I am angry with my selfe, now that I wake.

FERDINAND. Get thee into some unknowne part o'th' world
That I may never see thee.   BOSOLA. Let me know
Wherefore I should be thus neglected? sir,
I serv'd your tyranny: and rather strove,
To satisfie your selfe, then all the world;
And though I loath'd the evill, yet I lov'd
You that did councell it: and rather sought
To appeare a true servant, then an honest man.
        FERDINAND. I'll goe hunt the Badger, by Owle-light:
'Tis a deed of darkenesse.   [*exit*
        BOSOLA. He's much distracted: Off my painted honour!—
While with vaine hopes, our faculties we tyre,
We seeme to sweate in yce, and freeze in fire;
What would I doe, we[r]e this to doe againe?
I would not change my peace of conscience
For all the wealth of Europe: She stirres; here's life:
Returne (faire soule) from darkenes, and lead mine
Out of this sencible Hell: She's warme, she breathes:
Upon thy pale lips I will melt my heart
To store them with fresh colour: who's there?
Some cordiall drinke! Alas! I dare not call:
So, pitty would destroy pitty: her Eye opes,
And heaven in it seemes to ope, (that late was shut)
To take me up to mer[c]y.
        DUCHESS. *Antonio.*
        BOSOLA. Yes (Madam) he is living,
The dead bodies you saw, were but faign'd statues;
He's reconcil'd to your brothers: the Pope hath wrought
The attonement.
        DUCHESS. Mercy!   [*she dies*
        BOSOLA. Oh, she's gone againe: there the cords of life broake:
Oh sacred Innocence, that sweetely sleepes
On Turtles feathers: whil'st a guilty conscience
Is a blacke Register, wherein is writ
All our good deedes, and bad: a Perspective
That showes us hell; that we cannot be suffer'd
To doe good when we have a mind to it!
This is manly sorrow:
These teares, I am very certaine, never grew
In my Mothers Milke. My estate is suncke below
The degree of feare: where were these penitent fountaines,
While she was living?
Oh, they were frozen up: here is a sight

As direfull to my soule, as is the sword
Unto a wretch hath slaine his father: Come,
I'll beare thee hence,
And execute thy last will; that's deliver
Thy body to the reverend dispose
Of some good women: that the cruell tyrant
Shall not denie me: Then I'll poast to *Millaine*,
Where somewhat I will speedily enact
Worth my dejection.   *[exit [with the body]*

ACTUS V.   SCENA I

[*Milan*]

[*Enter Antonio and Delio*]

ANTONIO.   What thinke you of my hope of reconcilement
To the *Aragonian* brethren?   DELIO.   I misdoubt it,
For though they have sent their letters of safe conduct
For your repaire to *Millaine*, they appeare
But Nets, to entrap you: The Marquis of *Pescara*
Under whom you hold certaine land in Cheit,
Much 'gainst his noble nature, hath bin mov'd
To ceize those lands, and some of his dependants
Are at this instant, making it their suit
To be invested in your Revenewes.
I cannot thinke, they meane well to your life,
That doe deprive you of your meanes of life,
Your living.   ANTONIO.   You are still an heretique
To any safety, I can shape my selfe.

DELIO.   Here comes the Marquis: I will make my selfe
Petitioner for some part of your land,
To know wh[i]ther it is flying.   ANTONIO.   I pray doe.

[*enter Pescara: Antonio withdraws*

DELIO.   Sir, I have a suit to you.   PESCARA.   To me?
DELIO.   An easie one:
There is the Cittadell of St. *Bennet*,
With some demeasnes, of late in the possession
Of *Antonio Bologna*—please you bestow them on me?

PESCARA. You are my friend: But this is such a suit,
Nor fit for me to give, nor you to take.

DELIO. No sir?

PESCARA. I will give you ample reason for't,
Soone in private: Here's the Cardinalls Mistris.   [*enter Julia*

JULIA. My Lord, I am growne your poore Petitioner,
And should be an ill begger, had I not
A Great mans letter here, (the Cardinalls)
To Court you in my favour.   [*gives letter*

PESCARA. [*reads*] He entreates for you
The Cittadell of Saint *Bennet*, that belong'd
To the banish'd *Bologna*.   JULIA. Yes:

PESCARA. I could not have thought of a friend I could
Rather pleasure with it: 'tis yours:

JULIA. Sir, I thanke you:
And he shall know how doubly I am engag'd
Both in your guift, and speedinesse of giving,
Which makes your graunt, the greater.   [*exit*

ANTONIO. [*aside*] How they fortefie
Themselves with my ruine!   DELIO. Sir: I am
Litle bound to you: PESCARA. Why?

DELIO. Because you denide this suit, to me, and gav't
To such a creature.

PESCARA. Doe you know what it was?
It was *Antonios* land: not forfeyted
By course of lawe; but ravish'd from his throate
By the Cardinals entreaty: it were not fit
I should bestow so maine a peece of wrong
Upon my friend: 'tis a gratification
Onely due to a Strumpet: for it is injustice;
Shall I sprinckle the pure blood of Innocents
To make those followers, I call my friends
Looke ruddier upon me? I am glad
This land, (ta'ne from the owner by such wrong)
Returnes againe unto so fowle an use,
As Salary for his Lust. Learne, (good *Delio*)
To aske noble things of me, and you shall find
I'll be a noble giver.   DELIO. You instruct me well:

ANTONIO. [*aside*] Why, here's a man, now, would fright im-
      pudence
From sawciest Beggers.

PESCARA. Prince *Ferdinand's* come to *Millaine*
Sicke (as they give out) of an Appoplexie:

But some say, 'tis a frenzie; I am going
To visite him.   [*exit*

ANTONIO. 'Tis a noble old fellow:

DELIO. What course doe you meane to take, *Antonio?*

ANTONIO. This night, I meane to venture all my fortune
(Which is no more then a poore lingring life)
To the Cardinals worst of mallice: I have got
Private accesse to his chamber: and intend
To visit him, about the mid of night.
(As once his brother did our noble Dutchesse.)
It may be that the sudden apprehension
Of danger (for I'll goe in mine owne shape)
When he shall see it fraight with love, and dutie,
May draw the poyson out of him, and worke
A friendly reconcilement; if it faile...
Yet, it shall rid me of this infamous calling,
For better fall once, then be ever falling.

DELIO. I'll second you in all danger: and (how ere)
My life keepes rancke with yours.

ANTONIO. You are still my lov'd, and best friend.   [*exeunt*

SCENA II

[*Milan. The Palace of the Cardinal and Ferdinand*]

[*Enter Pescara and Doctor*]

PESCARA. Now Doctor; may I visit your Patient?

DOCTOR. If't please your Lordship: but he's instantly
To take the ayre here in the Gallery,
By my direction.

PESCARA. 'Pray-thee, what's his disease?

DOCTOR. A very pestilent disease (my Lord)
They call *Licanthropia.*   PESCARA. What's that?
I need a Dictionary to't.   DOCTOR. I'll tell you:
In those that are possess'd with't there ore-flowes
Such mellencholy humour, they imagine
Themselves to be transformed into Woolves,
Steale forth to Church-yards in the dead of night,
And dig dead bodies up: as two nights since
One met the Duke, 'bout midnight in a lane
Behind St. *Markes* Church, with the leg of a man
Upon his shoulder; and he howl'd fearefully:

Said he was a Woolffe: onely the difference
Was, a Woolffes skinne was hairy on the out-side,
His on the In-side: bad them take their swords,
Rip up his flesh, and trie: straight I was sent for,
And having ministerd to him, found his Grace
Very well recovered.   PESCARA. I am glad on't.
   DOCTOR. Yet not without some feare
Of a relaps: if he grow to his fit againe,
I'll goe a neerer way to worke with him
Then ever *Parac[el]sus* dream'd of: If
They'll give me leave, I'll buffet his madnesse out of him.
Stand aside: he comes.

   [Enter Ferdinand, Mallateste, Cardinal and Bosola]

   FERDINAND. Leave me.
   MALLATESTE. Why doth your Lordship love this solitarines?
   FERDINAND. Eagles commonly fly alone: They are Crowes,
Dawes, and Sterlings that flocke together: Looke, what's that,
followes me?   MALLATESTE. Nothing (my Lord).
   FERDINAND. Yes: MALLATESTE. 'Tis your shadow.
   FERDINAND. Stay it, let it not haunt me.
   MALLATESTE. Impossible; if you move, and the Sun shine:
   FERDINAND. I will throtle it.   *[throws himself on the ground*
   MALLATESTE. Oh, my Lord: you are angry with nothing.
   FERDINAND. You are a foole: How is't possible I should catch
my shadow unlesse I fall upon't? When I goe to Hell, I meane to
carry a bribe: for looke you good guifts ever-more make way, for
the worst persons.
   PESCARA. Rise, good my Lord.
   FERDINAND. I am studying the Art of Patience.
   PESCARA. 'Tis a noble Vertue;
   FERDINAND. To drive six Snailes before me, from this towne
to *Mosco*; neither use Goad, nor Whip to them, but let them take
their owne time: (the patientst man i'th' world match me for an
experiment) and I'll crawle after like a sheepe-biter.
   CARDINALL. Force him up.
   FERDINAND. Use me well, you were best:
What I have don, I have don: I'll confesse nothing.
   DOCTOR. Now let me come to him: Are you mad (my Lord?)
Are you out of your Princely wits?
   FERDINAND. What's he?   PESCARA. Your Doctor.
   FERDINAND. Let me have his beard saw'd off, and his eye-
      browes

Fil'd more civill.

DOCTOR. I must do mad trickes with him,
For that's the onely way on't. I have brought
Your grace a Salamanders skin, to keepe you
From sun-burning.

FERDINAND. I have cruell sore eyes.

DOCTOR. The white of a Cockatrixes-egge is present remedy.

FERDINAND. Let it be a new-layd one, you were best:
Hide me from him: Phisitians are like Kings,
They brooke no contradiction.

DOCTOR. Now he begins
To feare me, now let me alone with him.   [*takes off his gown*

CARDINALL. How now, put off your gowne?

DOCTOR. Let me have some forty urinalls fill'd with Rose-
water: He, and I'll go pelt one another with them—now he begins
to feare me: Can you fetch a friske, sir? Let him go, let him go,
upon my perrill: I finde by his eye, he stands in awe of me, I'll
make him—as tame as a Dormouse.

FERDINAND. Can you fetch your friskes, sir? I will stamp him
into a Cullice: Flea off his skin, to cover one of the An[a]tomies,
this rogue hath set i'th'cold yonder, in Barber-Chyrurgeons hall:
Hence, hence, you are all of you, like beasts for sacrifice, [*throws
the doctor down and beats him*] there's nothing left of you, but
tongue, and belly, flattery, and leachery.   [*exit*

PESCARA. Doctor, he did not feare you throughly.

DOCTOR. True, I was somewhat to[o] forward.

BOSOLA. Mercy upon me, what a fatall judgement
Hath falne upon this *Ferdinand*!

PESCARA. Knowes your grace
What accident hath brought unto the Prince
This strange distraction?

CARDINALL. [*aside*] I must faigne somewhat: Thus they say
    it grew.
You have heard it rumor'd for these many years,
None of our family dies, but there is seene
The shape of an old woman, which is given
By tradition, to us, to have bin murther'd
By her Nephewes, for her riches: Such a figure
One night (as the Prince sat up late at's booke,
Appear'd to him—when crying out for helpe,
The gentlemen of's chamber, found his grace
All on a cold sweate, alter'd much in face
And language: Since which apparition,

He hath growne worse, and worse, and I much feare
He cannot live.

    BOSOLA. Sir, I would speake with you.

    PESCARA. We'll leave your grace,
Wishing to the sicke Prince, our noble Lord,
All health of minde, and body.

    CARDINALL. You are most welcome:

                        [exeunt: manent Cardinal and Bosola

Are you come? so: [*aside*] this fellow must not know
By any meanes I had intelligence
In our Duchesse death: For (though I counsell'd it,)
The full of all th'ingagement seem'd to grow
From *Ferdinand*: [*to Bosola*] Now sir, how fares our sister?
I do not thinke but sorrow makes her looke
Like to an oft-di'd garment: She shall now
Tast comfort from me: why do you looke so wildely?
Oh, the fortune of your master here, the Prince
Dejects you—but be you of happy comfort:
If you'll do on[e] thing for me I'll entreate,
Though he had a cold tombe-stone ore his bones,
[I'll] make you what you would be.

    BOSOLA. Any thing—
Give it me in a breath, and let me flie to't:
They that thinke long, small expedition win,
For musing much o'th'end, cannot begin.   *[enter Julia*

    JULIA. Sir, will you come in to Supper?

    CARDINALL. I am busie, leave me.

    JULIA. [*aside*] What an excellent shape hath that fellow! *[exit*

    CARDINALL. 'Tis thus: *Antonio* lurkes here in *Millaine*,
Enquire him out, and kill him: while he lives,
Our sister cannot marry, and I have thought
Of an excellent match for her: do this, and stile me
Thy advancement.

    BOSOLA. But by what meanes shall I find him out?

    CARDINALL. There is a gentleman, call'd *Delio*
Here in the Campe, that hath bin long approv'd
His loyall friend: Set eie upon that fellow,
Follow him to Masse—may be *Antonio*,
Although he do account religion
But a Schoole-name, for fashion of the world,
May accompany him—or else go enquire out
Delio's Confessor, and see if you can bribe
Him to reveale it: there are a thousand wayes

A man might find to trace him: As to know,
What fellowes haunt the Jewes, for taking up
Great summes of money, for sure he's in want,
Or else to go to th'Picture-makers, and learne
Who [bought] her Picture lately—some of these
Happily may take——
    BOSOLA. Well, I'll not freeze i'th'businesse,
I would see that wretched thing, *Antonio*
Above all sightes i'th'world.
      CARDINALL. Do, and be happy.   [*exit*
    BOSOLA. This fellow doth breed Bazalisques in's eies,
He's nothing else, but murder: yet he seemes
Not to have notice of the Duchesse death:
'Tis his cunning: I must follow his example,
There cannot be a surer way to trace,
Then that of an old Fox.   [*enter Julia, pointing a pistol at him*
    JULIA. So, sir, you are well met.   BOSOLA. How now?
    JULIA. Nay, the doores are fast enough:
Now, Sir, I will make you confesse your treachery.
    BOSOLA. Treachery?   JULIA. Yes, confesse to me
Which of my women 'twas you hyr'd, to put
Love-powder into my drinke?
    BOSOLA. Love-powder?
    JULIA. Yes, when I was at *Malfy*—
Why should I fall in love with such a face else?
I have already suffer'd for thee so much paine,
The onely remedy to do me good,
Is to kill my longing.
    BOSOLA. Sure your Pistoll holds
Nothing but perfumes, or kissing comfits: excellent Lady,
You have a pritty way on't to discover
Your longing: Come, come, I'll disarme you,
And arme you thus—yet this is wondrous strange.   [*embraces her*
    JULIA. Compare thy forme, and my eyes together,
You'll find my love no such great miracle:
Now you'll say,
I am wanton: This nice modesty, in Ladies
Is but a troublesome familiar,
That haunts them.
    BOSOLA. Know you me, I am a blunt souldier.
    JULIA. The better,
Sure, there wants fire, where there are no lively sparkes
Of roughnes.   BOSOLA. And I want complement.

JULIA. Why, ignorance in court-ship cannot make you do
    amisse,
If you have a heart to do well.
    BOSOLA. You are very faire.
    JULIA. Nay, if you lay beauty to my charge,
I must plead unguilty.   BOSOLA. Your bright eyes
Carry a Quiver of darts in them, sharper
Then Sun-beames.
    JULIA. You will mar me with commendation,
Put your selfe to the charge of courting me,
Whereas now I wo[o] you.
    BOSOLA. [aside] I have it, I will worke upon this
      Creature—
Let us grow most amorously familiar:
If the great Cardinall now should see me thus,
Would he not count me a villaine?
    JULIA. No, he might count me a wanton,
Not lay a scruple of offence on you:
For if I see, and steale a Diamond,
The fault is not i'th'stone, but in me the thiefe,
That purloines it: I am sudaine with you—
We that are great women of pleasure, use to cut off
These uncertaine wishes, and unquiet longings,
And in an instant joyne the sweete delight
And the pritty excuse together: had you bin in'th'streete,
Under my chamber window, even there
I should have courted you.
    BOSOLA. Oh, you are an excellent Lady.
    JULIA. Bid me do somewhat for you presently,
To expresse I love you.
    BOSOLA. I will, and if you love me,
Faile not to effect it:
The Cardinall is growne wondrous mellancholly,
Demand the cause, let him not put you off,
With faign'd excuse, discover the maine ground on't.
    JULIA. Why would you know this?
    BOSOLA. I have depended on him,
And I heare that he is falne in some disgrace
With the Emperour—if he be, like the mice
That forsake falling houses, I would shift
To other dependance.
    JULIA. You shall not neede follow the warres,
I'll be your maintenance.

BOSOLA. And I your loyall servant,
But I cannot leave my calling.
    JULIA. Not leave an
Ungratefull Generall, for the love of a sweete Lady?
You are like some, cannot sleepe in feather-beds,
But must have blockes for their pillowes.
    BOSOLA. Will you do this?   JULIA. Cunningly.
    BOSOLA. To-morrow I'll expect th'intelligence.
    JULIA. To-morrow! get you into my Cabinet,
You shall have it with you: do not delay me,
No more then I do you: I am like one
That is condemn'd: I have my pardon promis'd.
But I would see it seal'd: Go, get you in,
You shall see me winde my tongue about his heart,
Like a skeine of silke.   [exit Bosola, into her cabinet: enter Cardinal
    CARDINALL. Where are you? [enter Servants.]
    SERVANT. Here.
    CARDINALL. Let none, upon your lives,
Have conference with the Prince Ferdinand,
Unlesse I knowe it: [aside] In this distraction   [exeunt Servants
He may reveale the murther:
Yond's my lingring consumption:
I am weary of her; and by any meanes
Would be quit off.   JULIA. How now, my Lord?
What ailes you?   CARDINALL. Nothing.
    JULIA. Oh, you are much alterd:
Come, I must be your Secretary, and remove
This lead from off your bosome, what's the matter?
    CARDINALL. I may not tell you.
    JULIA. Are you so farre in love with sorrow,
You cannot part with part of it? or thinke you
I cannot love your grace, when you are sad,
As well as merry? or do you suspect
I, that have bin a secret to your heart,
These many winters, cannot be the same
Unto your tongue?
    CARDINALL. Satisfie thy longing,
The onely way to make thee keepe my councell,
Is not to tell thee.   JULIA. Tell your eccho this,
Or flatterers, that (like ecchoes) still report
What they heare (though most imperfect), and not me:
For, if that you be true unto your selfe,
I'll know.   CARDINALL. Will you racke me?

JULIA. No, judgement shall
Draw it from you: It is an equall fault,
To tell ones secrets, unto all, or none.
    CARDINALL. The first argues folly.
    JULIA. But the last tyranny.
    CARDINALL. Very well; why, imagine I have committed
Some secret deed, which I desire the world
May never heare of.
    JULIA. Therefore may not I know it?
You have conceal'd for me, as great a sinne
As adultery: Sir, never was occasion
For perfect triall of my constancy
Till now: Sir, I beseech you.
    CARDINALL. You'll repent it.   JULIA. Never.
    CARDINALL. It hurries thee to ruine: I'll not tell thee—
Be well advis'd, and thinke what danger 'tis
To receive a Princes secrets: they that do,
Had neede have their breasts hoop'd with adamant
To containe them: I pray thee yet be satisfi'd,
Examine thine owne frailety, 'tis more easie
To tie knots, then unloose them: 'tis a secret
That (like a lingring poyson) may chance lie
Spread in thy vaines, and kill thee seaven yeare hence.
    JULIA. Now you dally with me.
    CARDINALL. No more—thou shalt know it.
By my appointment, the great Duchesse of *Malfy*,
And two of her yong children, foure nights since
Were strangled.
    JULIA. Oh heaven! (sir) what have you done?
    CARDINALL. How now? how setles this? thinke you your
        bosome
Will be a grave, darke and obscure enough
For such a secret?
    JULIA. You have undone your selfe (sir.)
    CARDINALL. Why?   JULIA. It lies not in me to conceale it.
    CARDINALL. No?
Come, I will sweare you to't upon this booke.
    JULIA. Most religiously.   CARDINALL. Kisse it.
Now you shall never utter it, thy curiosity
Hath undone thee: thou'rt poyson'd with that booke—
Because I knew thou couldst not keepe my councell,
I have bound the[e] to't by death.   *[enter Bosola*
    BOSOLA. For pitty sake, hold.   CARDINALL. Ha, *Bosola?*

JULIA. I forgive you
This equall peece of Justice you have done:
For I betraid your councell to that fellow,
He overheard it; that was the cause I said
It lay not in me, to conceale it.

BOSOLA. Oh foolish woman,
Couldst not thou have poyson'd him?

JULIA. 'Tis weakenesse,
Too much to thinke what should have bin done—I go,
I know not wh[i]ther.   [*dies*

CARDINALL. Wherefore com'st thou hither?

BOSOLA. That I might finde a great man, (like your selfe,)
Not out of his wits (as the Lord *Ferdinand*)
To remember my service.

CARDINALL. I'll have thee hew'd in peeces.

BOSOLA. Make not your selfe such a promise of that life
Which is not yours, to dispose of.

CARDINALL. Who plac'd thee here?

BOSOLA. Her lust, as she intended.

CARDINALL. Very well,
Now you know me for your fellow murderer.

BOSOLA. And wherefore should you lay faire marble colours,
Upon your rotten purposes to me?
Unlesse you imitate some that do plot great Treasons,
And when they have done, go hide themselves i'th'graves
Of those were Actors in't?   CARDINALL. No more,
There is a fortune attends thee.

BOSOLA. Shall I go sue to fortune any longer?
'Tis the fooles Pilgrimage.

CARDINALL. I have honors in store for thee.

BOSOLA. There are a many wayes that conduct to seeming
Honor, and some of them very durty ones.

CARDINALL. Throw to the divell
Thy mellancholly—the fire burnes well,
What neede we keepe a-stirring of't, and make
A greater smoother? thou wilt kill *Antonio*?

BOSOLA. Yes.   CARDINALL. Take up that body.

BOSOLA. I thinke I shall
Shortly grow the common B[ie]re, for Church-yards?

CARDINALL. I will allow thee some dozen of attendants,
To aide thee in the murther.

BOSOLA. Oh, by no meanes—Phisitians that apply horse-
leiches to any rancke swelling, use to cut of[f] their tailes, that the

blood may run through them the faster: Let me have no traine,
when I goe to shed blood, least it make me have a greater, when
I ride to the Gallowes.

CARDINALL. Come to me
After midnight, to helpe to remove that body
To her owne Lodging: I'll give out she dide o'th' Plague;
'Twill breed the lesse enquiry after her death.

BOSOLA. Where's *Castruchio*, her husband?

CARDINALL. He's rod[e] to *Naples* to take possession
Of *Antonio's* Cittadell.

BOSOLA. Beleeve me, you have done a very happy turne.

CARDINALL. Faile not to come: There is the Master-key
Of our Lodgings: and by that you may conceive
What trust I plant in you.

BOSOLA. You shall find me ready.   [*exit [Cardinal]*]
Oh poore *Antonio*, though nothing be so needfull
To thy estate, as pitty, Yet I finde
Nothing so dangerous: I must looke to my footing;
In such slippery yce-pavements, men had neede
To be frost-nayld well: they may breake their neckes else.
The Pre[ce]dent's here afore me: how this man
Beares up in blood!—seemes feareles!—why, 'tis well:
Securitie some men call the Suburbs of Hell,
Onely a dead wall betweene. Well (good *Antonio*)
I'll seeke thee out; and all my care shall be
To put thee into safety from the reach
Of these most cruell biters, that have got
Some of thy blood already. It may be,
I'll joyne with thee, in a most just revenge.
The weakest Arme is strong enough, that strikes
With the sword of Justice: Still me thinkes the Dutchesse
Haunts me: there, there!...'tis nothing but my mellancholy.
O Penitence, let me truely tast thy Cup,
That throwes men downe, onely to raise them up.   [*exit*

SCENA III

[Milan. Part of the fortification of the city]

[Enter Antonio and Delio. There is an] Eccho,
(from the Dutchesse Grave)

DELIO. Yond's the Cardinall's window: This fortification
Grew from the ruines of an auncient Abbey:
And to yond side o'th' river, lies a wall
(Peece of a Cloyster) which in my opinion
Gives the best Eccho, that you ever heard;
So hollow, and so dismall, and withall
So plaine in the destinction of our words,
That many have supposde it is a Spirit
That answeres.

ANTONIO. I doe love these auncient ruynes:
We never tread upon them, but we set
Our foote upon some reverend History.
And questionles, here in this open Court
(Which now lies naked to the injuries
Of stormy weather) some men lye Enterr'd
Lov'd the Church so well, and gave so largely to't,
They thought it should have canopide their Bones
Till Doombes-day: But all things have their end:
Churches, and Citties (which have diseases like to men)
Must have like death that we have.

ECCHO. *Like death that we have.*

DELIO. Now the *Eccho* hath caught you:

ANTONIO. It groan'd (me thought) and gave
A very deadly Accent?

ECCHO. *Deadly Accent.*

DELIO. I told you 'twas a pretty one: You may make it
A Huntes-man, or a Faulconer, a Musitian,
Or a Thing of Sorrow.

ECCHO. *A Thing of Sorrow.*

ANTONIO. I sure: that suites it best.

ECCHO. *That suites it best.*

ANTONIO. 'Tis very like my wi[ff]es voyce.

ECCHO. *I, wifes-voyce.*

DELIO. Come: let's walke farther from't:
I would not have you go to th' *Cardinalls* to-night:
Doe not.

ECCHO. *Doe not.*

DELIO. Wisdome doth not more moderate wasting Sorrow
Then time: take time for't: be mindfull of thy safety.

ECCHO. *Be mindfull of thy safety.*

ANTONIO. Necessitie compells me:
Make scruteny throughout the pass[ag]es
Of your owne life; you'll find it impossible
To flye your fate.

[ECCHO.] *O flye your fate.*

DELIO. Harke: the dead stones seeme to have pitty on you
And give you good counsell.

ANTONIO. *Eccho*, I will not talke with thee;
For thou art a dead Thing.

ECCHO. *Thou art a dead Thing.*

ANTONIO. My Dutchesse is asleepe now,
And her litle-Ones, I hope sweetly: oh Heaven
Shall I never see her more?

ECCHO. *Never see her more:*

ANTONIO. I mark'd not one repetition of the *Eccho*
But that: and on the sudden, a cleare light
Presented me a face folded in sorrow.

DELIO. Your fancy; meerely.

ANTONIO. Come: I'll be out of this Ague;
For to live thus, is not indeed to live:
It is a mockery, and abuse of life—
I will not henceforth save my selfe by halves,
Loose all, or nothing.

DELIO. Your owne vertue save you!
I'll fetch your eldest sonne; and second you:
It may be that the sight of his owne blood
Spred in so sweet a figure, may beget
The more compassion.

[ANTONIO.] How ever, fare you well:
Though in our miseries, Fortune have a part,
Yet, in our noble suffrings, she hath none—
Contempt of paine, that we may call our owne.   [*exeunt*

SCENA IIII

[Milan. The Palace of the Cardinal and Ferdinand]

*[Enter Cardinal, Pescara, Mallateste, Roderigo,
Grisolan]*

CARDINALL. You shall not watch to-night by the sicke Prince,
His Grace is very well recover'd.
    MALLATESTE. Good my Lord suffer us.
    CARDINALL. Oh, by no meanes:
The noyce, and change of object in his eye,
Doth more distract him: I pray, all to bed,
And though you heare him in his violent fit,
Do not rise, I intreate you.
    PESCARA. So, sir; we shall not—
    CARDINALL. Nay, I must have you promise
Upon your honors, for I was enjoyn'd to't
By himselfe; and he seem'd to urge it sencibly.
    PESCARA. Let ou[r] honors bind this trifle.
    CARDINALL. Nor any of your followers.
    MALLATESTE. Neither.
    CARDINALL. It may be, to make triall of your promise,
When he's asleepe, my selfe will rise, and faigne
Some of his mad trickes, and crie out for helpe,
And faigne my selfe in danger.
    MALLATESTE. If your throate were cutting,
I'll'd not come at you, now I have protested against it.
    CARDINALL. Why, I thanke you.   *[withdraws a little*
    GRISOLAN. 'Twas a foule storme to-night.
    RODERIGO. The Lord *Ferdinand's* chamber shooke like an
    Ozier.
    MALLATESTE. 'Twas nothing but pure kindnesse in the Divell,
To rocke his owne child.   *[exeunt [except Cardinal*
    CARDINALL. The reason why I would not suffer these
About my brother, is, because at midnight
I may with better privacy, convay
Julias body to her owne Lodging: O, my Conscience!
I would pray now: but the Divell takes away my heart
For having any confidence in Praier.
About this houre, I appointed *Bosola*
To fetch the body: when he hath serv'd my turne,
He dies.   *[exit: [enter Bosola*

BOSOLA. Hah? 'twas the Cardinalls voyce: I heard him name,
Bosola, and my death: listen, I heare ones footing.   [*enter*
FERDINAND. Strangling is a very quie[t] death.   *Ferdinand*
BOSOLA. Nay then I see, I must stand upon my Guard.
FERDINAND. What say' to that? whisper, softly: doe you
     agree to't?
So—it must be done i'th' darke: the Cardinall
Would not for a thousand pounds, the Doctor should see it.   [*exit*
BOSOLA. My death is plotted; here's the consequence of
     murther.
"*We value not desert, nor Christian breath,*
When we know blacke deedes must be cur'de with death.
                                   [*enter Antonio and Servant*
SERVANT. Here stay Sir, and be confident, I pray:
I'll fetch you a darke Lanthorne.   [*exit*
ANTONIO. Could I take him
At his prayers, there were hope of pardon.
BOSOLA. Fall right my sword: [*strikes him*
I'll not give thee so much leysure, as to pray.
ANTONIO. Oh, I am gone: Thou hast ended a long suit,
In a mynut.
BOSOLA. What art thou?
ANTONIO. A most wretched thing,
That onely have thy benefit in death,
To appeare my selfe.   [*re-enter Servant, with light*
SERVANT. Where are you Sir?
ANTONIO. Very neere my home: *Bosola?*
SERVANT. Oh misfortune!
BOSOLA. [*to the Servant*] Smother thy pitty, thou art dead else:
     Antonio?
The man I would have sav'de 'bove mine owne life!
We are meerely the Starres tennys-balls (strooke, and banded
Which way please them)—oh good *Antonio*,
I'll whisper one thing in thy dying eare,
Shall make thy heart breake quickly: Thy faire Dutchesse
And two sweet Children...
ANTONIO. Their very names
Kindle a litle life in me.
BOSOLA. Are murderd!
ANTONIO. Some men have wish'd to die,
At the hearing of sad tydings: I am glad
That I shall do't in sadnes: I would not now
Wish my wounds balm'de, nor heal'd: for I have no use

To put my life to: In all our Quest of Greatnes...
(Like wanton Boyes, whose pastime is their care)
We follow after bubbles, blowne in th'ayre.
Pleasure of life, what is't? onely the good houres
Of an Ague: meerely a preparative to rest,
To endure vexation: I doe not aske
The processe of my death: onely commend me
To *Delio*.
   BOSOLA. Breake heart!
   ANTONIO. And let my Sonne, flie the Courts of Princes.   [*dies*
   BOSOLA. Thou seem'st to have lov'd *Antonio*?
   SERVANT. I brought him hether,
To have reconcil'd him to the Cardinall.
   BOSOLA. I doe not aske thee that:
Take him up, if thou tender thine owne life,
And beare him, where the Lady *Julia*
Was wont to lodge: Oh, my fate moves swift.
I have this Cardinall in the forge already,
Now I'll bring him to th'hammer: (O direfull misprision:)
I will not Imitate things glorious,
No more then base: I'll be mine owne example.
On, on: and looke thou represent, for silence,
The thing thou bear'st.   [*exeunt*

SCENA V

[*The same*]

[*Enter*] *Cardinall* (*with a Booke*)

CARDINALL. I am puzzell'd in a question about hell:
He saies, in hell, there's one materiall fire,
And yet it shall not burne all men alike.
Lay him by: How tedious is a guilty conscience!
When I looke into the Fish-ponds, in my Garden,
Me thinkes I see a thing, arm'd with a Rake
That seemes to strike at me:
              [*enter Bosola and Servant bearing Antonio's body*
Now? art thou come? thou look'st ghastly:
There sits in thy face, some great determination,
Mix'd with some feare.
   BOSOLA. Thus it lightens into Action:
I am come to kill thee.

CARDINALL. Hah? helpe! our Guard!

BOSOLA. Thou art deceiv'd:
They are out of thy howling.

CARDINALL. Hold: and I will faithfully devide
Revenewes with thee.

BOSOLA. Thy prayers, and proffers
Are both unseasonable.

CARDINALL. Raise the Watch:
We are betraid.

BOSOLA. I have confinde your flight:
I'll suffer your retreyt to *Julias* Chamber,
But no further.

CARDINALL. Helpe: we are betraid! [*enter Malateste, Roderigo,*
MALLATESTE. Listen: *Pescara, Grisolan, above*

CARDINALL. My Dukedome, for rescew!

RODERIGO. Fye upon his counterfeyting!

MALLATESTE. Why, 'tis not the Cardinall.

RODERIGO. Yes, yes, 'tis he:
But I'll see him hang'd, ere I'll goe downe to him.

CARDINALL. Here's a plot upon me, I am assaulted: I am lost,
Unlesse some rescew.

GRISOLAN. He doth this pretty well:
But it will not serve; to laugh me out of mine honour!

CARDINALL. The sword's at my throat:

RODERIGO. You would not bawle so lowd then.

MALLATESTE. Come, come: [let]'s goe to bed: he told us thus
    much aforehand.

PESCARA. He wish'd you should not come at him: but beleev't,
The accent of the voyce sounds not in jest.
I'll downe to him, howsoever, and with engines
Force ope the doores.   [*exit above*

RODERIGO. Let's follow him aloofe,
And note how the Cardinall will laugh at him.   [*exeunt above*

BOSOLA. There's for you first: 'cause you shall not unbarracade
The doore to let in rescew.   [*he kills the Servant*

CARDINALL. What cause hast thou
To pursue my life?

BOSOLA. Looke there:

CARDINALL. *Antonio?*

BOSOLA. Slaine by my hand unwittingly:
Pray, and be sudden: when thou kill'dst thy sister,
Thou tookst from Justice her most equall ballance,
And left her naught but her sword.

CARDINALL. O mercy!

BOSOLA. Now it seemes thy Greatnes was onely outward:
For thou fall'st faster of thy selfe, then calamitie
Can drive thee: I'll not wast longer time: There.   [*wounds him*

CARDINALL. Thou hast hurt me:

BOSOLA. Againe:

CARDINALL. Shall I die like a Levoret
Without any resistance? helpe, helpe, helpe:
I am slaine.   [*enter Ferdinand*

FERDINAND. Th'allarum? give me a fresh horse:
Rally the vaunt-guard: or the day is lost:
Yeeld, yeeld: I give you the honour of Armes,
Shake my Sword over you—will you yeilde?

CARDINALL. Helpe me, I am your brother.

FERDINAND. The divell?
My brother fight upon the adverse party?   [*he wounds the Car-*
There flies your ransome.   *dinall, and (in the scuffle) gives*

CARDINALL. Oh Justice: *Bosola his death wound*
I suffer now, for what hath former bin:
"Sorrow is held the eldest child of sin.

FERDINAND. Now you're brave fellowes: *Cæsars* Fortune was
harder then *Pompeys*: *Cæsar* died in the armes of prosperity,
Pompey at the feete of disgrace: you both died in the field—the
paine's nothing: paine many times is taken away with the apprehension of greater, (as the tooth-ache with the sight of a Barbor,
that comes to pull it out) there's Philosophy for you.

BOSOLA. Now my revenge is perfect: sinke (thou maine
   cause
Of my undoing)—the last part of my life,
Hath done me best service.   [*he kills Ferdinand*

FERDINAND. Give me some wet hay, I am broken-winded—
I do account this world but a dog-kennell:
I will vault credit, and affect high pleasures,
Beyond death.

BOSOLA. He seemes to come to himselfe,
Now he's so neere the bottom.

FERDINAND. My sister, oh! my sister, there's the cause on't.
"Whether we fall by ambition, blood, or lust,
"Like Diamonds, we are cut with our owne dust.   [*dies*

CARDINALL. Thou hast thy payment too.

BOSOLA. Yes, I hold my weary soule in my teeth,
'Tis ready to part from me: I do glory
That thou, which stood'st like a huge Piramid

Begun upon a large, and ample base,
Shalt end in a little point, a kind of nothing.

           [enter Pescara, Malateste, Roderigo and Grisolan

PESCARA. How now (my Lord?)

MALLATESTE. Oh sad disastre!

RODERIGO. How comes this?

BOSOLA. Revenge, for the Duchesse of *Malfy*, murdered
By th'*Aragonian* brethren: for *Antonio*,
Slaine by [t]his hand: for lustfull *Julia*,
Poyson'd by this man: and lastly, for my selfe,
(That was an Actor in the maine of all,
Much 'gainst mine owne good nature, yet i'th'end
Neglected.)

PESCARA. How now (my Lord?)

CARDINALL. Looke to my brother:
He gave us these large wounds, as we were strugling
Here i'th' rushes: And now, I pray, let me
Be layd by, and never thought of.   *[dies*

PESCARA. How fatally (it seemes) he did withstand
His owne rescew!

MALLATESTE. Thou wretched thing of blood,
How came *Antonio* by his death?

BOSOLA. In a mist: I know not how,
Such a mistake, as I have often seene
In a play: Oh, I am gone—
We are onely like dead wals, or vaulted graves,
That ruin'd, yeildes no eccho: Fare you well—
It may be paine: but no harme to me to die,
In so good a quarrell: Oh this gloomy world,
In what a shadow, or deepe pit of darknesse,
Doth (womanish, and fearefull) mankind live!
Let worthy mindes nere stagger in distrust
To suffer death, or shame, for what is just—
Mine is another voyage.   *[dies*

PESCARA. The noble *Delio*, as I came to th'Pallace,
Told me of *Antonio's* being here, and shew'd me
A pritty gentleman his sonne and heire.

           [enter Delio with Antonio's Son

MALLATESTE. Oh Sir, you come to[o] late.

DELIO. I heard so, and
Was arm'd for't ere I came: Let us make noble use
Of this great ruine; and joyne all our force
To establish this yong hopefull Gentleman

In's mothers right. These wretched eminent things
Leave no more fame behind 'em, then should one
Fall in a frost, and leave his print in snow—
As soone as the sun shines, it ever melts,
Both forme, and matter: I have ever thought
Nature doth nothing so great, for great men,
As when she's pleas'd to make them Lords of truth:
   "Integrity of life, is fames best friend,
   Which noblely (beyond Death) shall crowne the end.   *[exeunt*

FINIS